Early Celtic Versecraft

James Travis

Early
Celtic Versecraft

origin

development

diffusion

CORNELL UNIVERSITY PRESS

Ithaca, New York

First published 1973 by Cornell University Press.

This edition is not for sale in Ireland, Great Britain, and British Commonwealth countries.

International Standard Book Number 0–8014–0700–1
Library of Congress Catalog Card Number 71–184000

PRINTED IN THE REPUBLIC OF IRELAND

Contents

Preface vii

Abbreviations ix

Part I: Structure

  1 Rhythm and Form 1

  2 Paragraph and Stanza 22

Part II: Ornament

  3 Styles and Chronology 42

  4 Rules 45

  5 Incidence 50

  6 Hiberno-Latin Verse Ornament 68

  7 Derivation 86

Part III: Theories of Latin Derivation 97

  8 Structure 99

  9 Ornament 109

Part IV: Proliferation and Diffusion

  10 Proliferation 113

  11 Diffusion 118

Part V: Conclusion 151

Notes 157

Indexes 162

Preface

Early Celtic Versecraft verifies the continuity of Irish and Welsh poetic art from indigenous origins, despite such irruptions as the advent of Latin language and religion in the Western Isles. In this respect, *Early Celtic Versecraft* sustains the trend towards the vindication of Celtic origins, contributions and cultural continuity established by such publications as Françoise Henry's *Irish Art in the Early Christian Period*, Kathleen Hughes' *The Church in Early Irish Society*, Máire and Liam de Paor's *Early Christian Ireland*, D. A. Binchy's studies in early Irish law, Calvert Watkins' 'Indo-European Metrics and Archaic Irish Verse' (*Celtica* 6), James Carney's *Studies in Irish Literature and History*, and my *Miscellanea Musica Celtica*.

In verifying the indigenous origin of Celtic versecraft and the contours of its early development, I necessarily delineate in great detail its varieties of rhythm and form, and its subtleties of ornament. A prime concern is the nature and evolution of Celtic versecraft from the onset of strong speech stress. The exposition of course emphasizes significant data previously ignored or misinterpreted, and facts that offset theories. Work already well done is, however, taken as given—notably Watkins' correlation of archaic Irish verse lines with Indo-European analogues and archetypes. References to standard compendia are held to a minimum.

As regards the diffusion of Celtic versecraft, only the essentials are considered—those that correct or sharpen concepts currently enshrined in standard histories or other compendia, or that point to areas inviting detailed investigation by students of comparative literature. We are not attempting a history of Celtic verse, but rather the preliminary to history: analysis and rationalization of evidence, and the establishment of valid perspectives.

If *Early Celtic Versecraft* should lead some disciple of Ogmios a step or two closer to the god's interior shrine, let him be grateful to Dr Marion deNonie Barber, whose insistence on the niceties of manuscript preparation surely has gladdened our publishers, and whose counsel has spared the reader one-knows-not-what infelicities of expression; and to Professor C. W. Dunn, Head of the Department of Celtic Languages and Literature at Harvard University, whose encouragement at a critical juncture helped rekindle a flame that had flickered low.

Researching the Celtic past in isolation for some decades while occupied also in little ways with industrial and aerospace affairs, we were sustained by the fitful vision of a completed task that would be of some use to scholars more fortunately placed and more ideally prepared. By the same token, we have enjoyed the grim solace that inadequacies of effort or fulfilment, such as they might be, would be our own.

JAMES TRAVIS

Tulsa, Oklahoma, 1942

Tuscaloosa, Alabama, 1972

Abbreviations

AB *The Antiphonary of Bangor.* Edited by F. E. Warren. London, 1895

BACC 'The Bodleian *Amra Choluimb Chille*'. Edited by W. Stokes. *Revue Celtique* XX (1899)

BCR *La Chanson de Roland.* Edited by J. Bedier. Paris, 1924

CA *Canu Aneirin.* Edited by Ifor Williams. Cardiff, 1938

CEIS Kathleen Hughes. *The Church in Early Irish Society.* Ithaca, New York: Cornell University Press, 1966

CLH *Canu Llywarch Hen.* Edited by Ifor Williams. Cardiff, 1935

CSIH James Carney. *Studies in Irish Literature and History.* Dublin, 1955

DLHR J. W. Duff. *A Literary History of Rome.* Third edition, second corrected impression. London, 1960

EPP *Encyclopedia of Poetry and Poetics.* Edited by Preminger. Princeton, 1963

GL *Gilgamesh.* Rendered in free rhythms by William Leonard. New York, 1934

HDV Andreas Heusler. 'Deutsche Versegeschichte'. In *Paul's Grundriss.* Berlin and Leipzig, 1925

HIEP Françoise Henry. *Irish Art in the Early Christian Period, to 800* A.D. Ithaca, New York: Cornell University Press, 1965

HLHI Douglas Hyde. *A Literary History of Ireland.* New edition, edited by Brian Ó Cuív. London, 1967

JAWS T. Gwynn Jones. 'Alliteration: Welsh and Scandinavian'. *Aberystwyth Studies* XIII (1934)

LH *The Irish Liber Hymnorum.* Edited by J. H. Bernard and R. Atkinson. London, 1898

LITL Kuno Meyer. *Learning in Ireland in the Fifth Century and the Transmission of Letters.* Dublin, 1913

MAID Kuno Meyer. 'Über die älteste irische Dichtung'. In *Abhandlungen der Königlich Preussischen Akademie der Wissenschaften, 1913, philosophisch-historische Klasse.* Berlin, 1914

MEIM   Gerard Murphy. *Early Irish Metrics*. Dublin, 1961

MMC   James Travis. *Miscellanea Musica Celtica*. New York: The Institute of Mediaeval Music, 1968

MMH   Kuno Meyer. 'Miscellanea Hibernica'. *University of Illinois Studies in Language and Literature* II (1916)

MPIM   Kuno Meyer. *A Primer of Irish Metrics*. Dublin, 1909

MSLI   R. A. S. Macalister. *The Secret Languages of Ireland*. Cambridge, 1937

OSHI   Frank O'Connor. *A Short History of Irish Literature: A Backward Look*. New York, 1967

PLRP   K. Polheim. *Die lateinische Reimprosa*. Berlin, 1925

QFC   Buell H. Quain. *The Flight of the Chiefs: Epic Poetry of the Fiji*. New York, 1942

RCLP   F. J. E. Raby. *A History of Christian Latin Poetry*. Oxford, 1927

RSLP   F. J. E. Raby. *A History of Secular Latin Poetry in the Middle Ages*. Second edition. Oxford, 1957

SESS   George Sigerson. *The Easter Song of Sedulius*. Dublin, 1922

STP   *Thesaurus Palaeohibernicus*. Edited by W. Stokes and J. Strachan. Cambridge, 1903

TBC   *Táin Bó Cúalgne*. Edited by Ernst Windisch. Leipzig, 1905

TIAV   Rudolf Thurneysen. 'Zur irischen Accent und Verslehre'. *Revue Celtique* VI (1885): 309–47

TIRC   James Travis. 'Intralinear Rhyme and Consonance in Early Celtic and Early Germanic Poetry'. *Germanic Review* XVIII, 2 (New York: Columbia University, 1943): 136–46

TMIV   Rudolf Thurneysen. 'Mittelirische Verslehren'. *Irische Texte* vol. III (Leipzig, 1891)

TPPD   James Travis. 'Parallels in Poetic Device between the Old French Epic and the Old Welsh Elegy'. *Publications of the Modern Language Association* LIX (New York, 1944): 1–6

VM   *Virgilii Maronis Grammatici Opera*. Edited by J. Heumer. Leipzig, 1884

WIEM   Calvert Watkins. 'Indo-European Metrics and Archaic Irish Verse'. *Celtica* VI (1963)

Part I : Structure

I

Rhythm and Form

Early Celtic sources preserve relatively archaic verse rhythms and forms juxtaposed with later forms. All the forms, being mature, indicate extensive development before their earliest documentation. The older rhythms and forms continued in use because their practitioners were august and their subject matter important: the pseudo-historical personages and events of sagas; the particulars of traditional law and genealogies; the efficacies of shamanistic ritual, magic, prayer and curse. In consequence of our sketching the characteristics, affiliations and evolution of early Celtic verse forms, the hitherto prevailing hypothesis of a Latin derivation for Old Irish stanzaic forms will be seen as not required; although the prestige that this concept has enjoyed for so long justifies its formal refutation.

A concern with the evolution of early Celtic verse forms tempts one to consider the origin of verse forms generally, and hence to examine the incidence of repetition, contrast and symmetry in the processes of nature and in the nature and activities of man. Such examination is deferred, however, as requiring extended separate analysis, especially of evidence not primarily literary; whereas it is possible, on literary evidence alone, to outline an organic development of Celtic verse lines from Indo-European archetypes. Yet a regard for the literary evidence need not entirely obscure the efficacy of utilitarian influence in assisting the regulation of verse rhythms and the configuring of verse forms: rhythmic regularity in vocal utterance, for example, tends to be induced not only by the rhythms of dance, march and song, but also by the intrinsic patterns of collective occupational, educational and ritualistic activities; of maternal lullaby; and of shamanistic magic, invocation and curse.

1

In early attempts to account for the character of Celtic verse forms—as by Ebel, Thurneysen, Kuno Meyer, Wilhelm Meyer aus Speyer, Zimmer, and their followers—indigenous propensities toward the regulation of vocal utterance tended to be disregarded. On the other hand, some ingenuity was devoted by these German scholars to attempting the derivation of Old Irish verse forms and ornament from Latin sources. At the time of these early attempts, the character of non-European verse was largely unknown to European philologists. Incontestable evidence of the independent generation of similar verse forms and ornament among disparate, unaffiliated cultures (whether advanced or primitive) was only beginning to come to light. The comparable elements of independently developed verse systems had been little noticed. Even so, such elements encompass every major aspect of verse structure and ornament: rhythms, the verse paragraph, the stanza (both quatrain and triad), incremental repetition, alliteration, assonance, and rime. For example, Egyptian verse by 2000 BC exhibits an artistic use of the incremental repetition and triadic stanza characteristic of early Welsh verse; Chinese verse by the fifth century BC exhibits regular quatrains, patterned end-rime, regular *word foot* rhythm, and various other parallels with early Irish verse; Ethiopian verse by the fifth century AD exhibits a unique kind of rime; Fiji verse exhibits a use of repetition not unlike that of ancient Babylonian verse, and also a systematic use of end assonance that compares with usage in the Old French *laisse*, the Old Spanish *juglar* and the early Welsh verse paragraphs. One could cite further parallels from poetries so mutually remote as the Hebrew, the Eskimo and the Japanese.[1] There is thus no more inherent necessity to seek a non-Celtic source for Celtic verse forms and ornament than for Celtic languages. It remains only to indicate the development of Celtic forms and ornament from their elements.

Rhythmic Regulation

Early Germanic, Celtic and Italic poetries disclose a style, broadly common, whose structure derives from stress: a typical verse unit, paired stresses; a typical verse line, paired units:

> *Hy*ge sceal be *heard*ra, *heor*te be cenre;
> *Mod* sceal be *ma*ra, be ure *mae*gen lytlab.
>
> —*Battle of Maldon,* lines 312–313[2]

Eo Rossa, roth ruirech,
recht flatha, fūaimm tuinne,
dech dūilib, dīriuch dronchrand,
dīa dronbalc, dorus nime.

—Old Irish panegyric (MPIM, p. 2)

uti tu morbos visos invisosque,
  viduertatem vastitudinemque,
calamitates intemperiasque
  prohibessis defendas averruncesque;
utique tu fruges, frumenta, vineta virgultaque
  grandire beneque evenire siris,
pastores pecuaque salva servassis
  duisque bonam salutem valetudinemque
mihi domo familiaeque nostrae.

—Prayer to Mars[3]

This basic structural pattern persisted in Germanic *alliterative accentual* verse from its earliest documentation to its final utterances a millennium later. In Celtic, the pattern persisted side by side with others. In Latin the pattern persisted as a mode of popular verse, although eventually assimilated to Grecian metres for learned poetry.

In all three poetries, rhythmic requirements were initially satisfied by the paired incidence of strong stresses—weak stresses being controlled by euphony rather than measure. Germanic verse structure, throughout its history, retained this relative flexibility in stress rhythm. Early Celtic and Italic poetries, on the other hand, disclose various modes of more rigid rhythmic regulation. Early Italic regulative modes are reflected in the Saturnian metre.[4] Early Celtic regulative modes survive in a variety that encompasses both the traits shared with early Italic and Germanic versifications and the traits distinctively Celtic.

Primal rhythmic concepts long preceded the emergence of a familiar analytic generalization—the *verse foot* of classical prosody. The *word foot* and the *word measure* first regulated the rhythm of Celtic and Italic verse units and verse lines.[5]

The *word foot*—defined as a word containing at least one strong (acute) stress—serves in Old Irish verse as a prime rhythmic element. In languages such as Old Irish and Old Latin, in which

words typically contain no more than three syllables, and more
often two, verse units made up of *word feet* consist typically of
paired words, each bearing one strong stress and an average of
one weak stress.   Pairs of such units produce a verse line euphonious
in stress rhythm, roughly regular in the incidence of its stresses,
and normative in the total number of its stresses (and hence of
its syllables).   In charms and incantations, however, a three-word
unit is common.   (See *Amorgen's Incantation*, p. 6 below.)

> Ēnna Labraid/lūad cāich,
> comarc Bresail/būain blāith.

> Brīg fēig/Fīachach fāth,
> ferr clū/Cathāir cāch.

> Cathach decheng/dāna fīal
> Fedelmid clothach/Corbmac cīar.   MAID, I, p. 27

> Hiberno puluere, uerno luto,
> Grandia farra, camille, metes.   DLHR, p. 59

> Postremus loquaris, primus taceas.   DLHR, p. 59

> Huat hanat huat; ista pista sista;
> Domiabo damna ustra.   DLHR,   p. 58

> > —charm for sprain

> Terra pestem teneto: salus hic maneto.   DLHR,   p. 58

> > —charm for foot pain

Word foot rhythm can be regulated by repeating *word foot* patterns,
by varying them, or by combining repetition and variation.   The
stress pattern of the two words that make up the *word foot* dimeter
can be repeated by word pairs throughout a poem, a verse paragraph
or a stanza.   For rhythmic variation (which in particular poems
may be preferred to rhythmic repetition) the stress pattern can be
changed in either or both of the paired words that make up the
dimeter.   These modes of rhythm can vary as to their types of
measure or regulation.

Within the basic *word foot* dimeter of paired stresses, the stresses may be provided by a pair of monosyllables:

Brig feig

by a monosyllable and a dissyllable (or polysyllable):

roth ruirech
Fiachach fath
mal adrualaid

by two dissyllables:

diriuch dronchrand
Enna Labraid

or by a dissyllable and a polysyllable; or by two polysyllables:

Fedelmid clothach
testidib tetbroga

The three stanzas (*Enna Labraid* etc.) quoted on p. 4, above, exhibit three frequently encountered varieties of *word foot* rhythm. Further, their rhythms are regulated: each pair of long lines has its own distinctive incidence of stress and word length. These regulatory procedures are exemplified in surviving Old Irish verse.

Repetition of the same *word foot* pattern throughout a poem results not only in absolute regularity of rhythm but also in uniformity of the number of syllables per verse unit. Repetition of a grammatical formula may entail the repetition of a *word foot* pattern, as in *Amorgen's Hymn* (dissyllables throughout):

Amgaeth i*m*muir   amtonn terthai*n*
amfuam i*m*muir   amdam setham
amséig foraill   amder gréne
amcain lubai   am hé illind.
amloch imaig   ambri dane

amgae lafodb feras fechtu
amde delbas do-chínd cotnu
cóiche nodgleid clochor slebe
cian cotgair aesa aisci
ciadu illaig fuiniud gréne   TMIV,   p. 61[6]

Such repetition of pattern may involve *conachlonn*—the repetition
of the last word of one verse line as the first word of the next—
as in *Amorgen's Incantation* (three-word lines throughout):]

Ailim iath n-erend
Ermac muir motach
Motach sliab sreatach
Sreatach coill ciotach
Ciotach ab eascach
Eascach loc lindmar
Lindmar tor tiopra
Tiopra tuath aenach
Aenach righ teamra
Teamair tor tuatach
Tuata mac milead
Mile long libearn
Libearn ard Ere
Ere ard diclass
Eber dond digbas
Diceadal ro gaet
Ro gaet ban breissi
Breissi ban buaich
[Be nadbail heriu]
Herimon ortus [hir]
hir Eber ailseas
Ailim iath n-erend[7]

Incremental repetition combined with *conachlonn* produces a
procession of paired dissyllables (with rhythmic expansion in the
last three lines):

Móra maitne
maitne Mide.
móra ossud
(ossud) Cullend.

móra cundscliu.
cundscliu Chlathra.
móra echrad.
echrad Assail.
móra tedmand.
tedmand tuath Bressi.
móra in chlóe
clóe Ulad im Chonchobar.   TBC,   p. 707

The *regulated word foot*, involving a use of *word feet* identically
structured as to strong and weak stresses, necessarily results in
verse units and verse lines whose stress rhythm, and indeed whose
total stress (and hence syllable) count, is quite uniform.

The *word measure*, defined as a word containing at least one
strong (acute) stress and two other stresses (at least one weak or
grave), occurs as a verse unit in lieu of the *word foot* dimeter. From
the outset of documentation, *word measure* occurs both in paired
rhythmic units and in only the second measure of dimeters. Here
it occurs in only the second measure, the first measure in each line
displaying *word foot* rhythm:

Cētach conn na crīche-se
fergein cotreb cutulsa
cētgein amra aithremail
āige agmar ollēchtach
maccām mīadach mōrfine
druimm fri dāma derbfine
ruiri Raigne rōtglaisse   MAID,   II, p. 6

Word measure could have emerged as conscious craft coincidently
with the use of regulated *word feet*. Dimeters composed of a two-
stress and a one-stress *word foot* would readily be taken to equate
with a three-stress *word measure*. For example, the first twelve
lines of the following Old Irish poem disclose *word foot* dimeters
regulated preponderantly to three stresses (two strong, one weak)
whereas, in the last two lines, a three-stress word provides the
rhythmic measure:

Crenaid brain
braigde fer
bruinden fuil

> feochair cath
> coinmid luind
> mesctuich tuind
> taib imthuill
> im nithgalaib
> iar luimnich
> luud fianna
> fetal ferda
> fir Cruachan
> cotas-crith
> immardbith.   TBC,   p. 831

Notice that, in the first six lines, the one-stress *word foot* ends the verse line and that, in the second six lines, the verse line usually begins with the one-stress *word foot*. The consequent difference in rhythm between the first and second six-line groups would seem to be an intended variation, and certainly a demonstration of one of the kinds of rhythmic enrichment that the regulated *word foot* can provide.

The archaic character of *word measure* rhythm is attested by Old Latin verse. In these lines from the *Carmen Arvale*, the first half of the verse line employs *word foot* rhythm; and the second, *word measure*:

> Enos Lases iuuate
>
> Enos Marmar iuuato   DLHR,   p. 58

Word measure rhythm, in Old Latin, occurs also in both halves of the long line:

> Semunis alternei   aduocapit conctos   DLHR,   p. 58

Word measure rhythm entails typically a uniform stress and hence syllable count within the *word measure*. Where *word measure* rhythm pervades both the short verse and the long verse, a line uniform in stress and hence syllable count necessarily characterizes the verse paragraph. Where *word measure* prevails in only the second (closing) measure of the line, the verse-end will be uniform in stress and hence syllable count.

Within the basic *word measure* dimeter, some variety of rhythmic effect is achieved, by regulation of the rhythm of word pairs: *word foot* measures composed of monosyllables and dissyllables are readily assimilable to *word measure* rhythm, as may be seen both in *Crenaid brain* (pp. 7-8, above) and in the following quatrain:

> Labraid lūam na lergge,
> faglaid fri fūam fairgge,
> glass glūairgrinn fri gente,
> blass būainbinn na bairddne.

$$(6^2 + 6^2) \text{ MAID I}, \quad \text{p. 6, fn. 1}$$

Use of *word measure* obviously provides strong diaeresis at the close of the verse unit and the verse line.

Rhythm varies frequently within the early quatrains but in a manner typically systematic, involving (1) change of rhythm between the first and second parts of the short line, and (2) recurrent change of rhythmic pattern between the first and second parts of the long line. These rhythmic differences often result in symmetrical differences between the total syllable count of the verse units involved, such that the quatrain may be assigned a signature according to its syllable count (or its syllabic structure). Such signatures, which we have indicated for various quatrains quoted herein, should not be permitted to obscure either the existence of their rhythmic basis or the rhythmic variety of lines whose syllable count may be identical. Obviously, the long couplets or the quatrains that display a regular arrangement or variation of rhythmic measure can be mistaken for syllabic verse by syllable counters unaware of Celtic rhythms:

> Māl adrūalaid īatha marb/macc sōēr Sētnī,
> selaig srathu Fomoire/for dōine domnaib.

$$(7^1 + 5^1) \text{ MAID II}, \quad \text{p. 6}$$

> Ōr ōs grēin gelmair/gabais for dōine domnaib
> sceo dēib, dīa ōin/as Mōin macc Āini ōinrīg.

$$(5^1 + 7^1) \text{ MAID II}, \quad \text{p. 10}$$

The following quatrain discloses complete rhythmic correspondence between the second and third lines, and between the opening measures of the first and fourth lines:

> Māir drecain dā Ēnna,
> aui nīthaig Nūadat,
> nascad gīallu Gōidel
> co nertmar Necht.
>
> $(6^3 + 4^1)$ MAID, II,   p. 19

Regulated *word foot* and *word measure* rhythms produce verse-ends that, depending on the particular stress pattern, may be monosyllabic, dissyllabic or trisyllabic.

The rhythm of the regulated *word measure* determines the trisyllabic character of the verse-ends of the rimeless *Cetach conn na crich-se* (p. 7) and of *Coimdiu caid cumachtach,* which is uniform in the syllabic length of both verse-end and verse line yet shows regular rime between only the closing verse ends of the two stanzas:

> Coimdiu cāid cumachtach,
> Crīst cain, ar clothbile,
> comarba nōibnime,
> nertaid fīal fīrinne,
> fri ferba fāth. $(6^4 + 4^1)$

> mac Maire ingine,
> Īsu ard airechda,
> ar n-ardflaith oirdnide,
> ri betha ic breithemnas
> ar brīg do brāth.   MPIM,   pp.24-25

The same rhythm pervades a quatrain quoted in its Irish source to illustrate one of the verse forms existing from pagan times and proper to the learned poets (*filid*):

> [N]imthang tadg torbathar
> testidib tétbroga
> breg dobre brígbrechtaib
> brigtar bronni bru. $(6^3 + 5^1)$ TMIV,   p. 35

Word measure rhythm occurs also in the *Martyrology of Oengus*:

> Sen a Christ mo labrai
> A choimmdiu secht nime
> Dom berthar buaid lere
> A ri grene gile. $(6^2 + 6^2)^8$

In all three instances just noted, the syllabic length of the verse line is a secondary consequence of *word measure* rhythm, rather than the prime determinant of verse structure or form.

Kuno Meyer cites various Old Irish poems to illustrate a supposed 'law' requiring a dissyllabic word as the final element in each half-line (or measure):

> Fo-chén Cét,
> Cét mac Mágach,
> mágen chúrad,
> críde n-éga,
> éithre n-éla,
> éirr trēn tréssa,
> tréthan ágach,
> cáin tárb tnúthach,
> Cét mac Mágach. MPIM, p. 2

> Fo-chén Lábraid
> lúathlām ar chláideb,
> láichdu ócaib,
> úallchu múrib!
> Mánnraid góssa,
> gníid cáthu,
> críathraid ócu,
> tócbaid lóbru,
> táirnid tríunu,
> fo-chén Lábraid! MPIM, p. 2

Here again the rhythm of the regulated *word foot* results in syllabic uniformity as a secondary consequence. The primary factor is stress rhythm: four regulated *word feet* to the long line, two to the half line, with link alliteration typically binding the end of one measure with the beginning of the next.

   Monosyllabic verse-ends occur in Old Irish verse, whether rimed
or rimeless, and in verse lines as short as three syllables or as long
as nine. In the oldest forms, the monosyllabic verse-end reflects
either *word foot* or *word measure* rhythm. In forms whose verse
line is short, the two *word feet* that make up the line tend to be
regulated, for uniformity of stress pattern; and this regulation
has as a secondary consequence lines typically uniform in syllabic
length. The monosyllabic verse-end occurs with perfect regularity
in the following poem (*fa-* in the fourth line apparently being a
prefix). The first word of the two-word line is obviously also
regulated in rhythm (and hence syllabically).

> Iasccach múir
> mothach tír
> tomaid*m* neisc
> iasc fathúind
> irathaib en
> fairrge cruaidh
> cassáir fínd
> crectaibh laigh
> leathai*n* mil
> *f*orta*ch*t laigh
> mniportach lugh
> todhmaid*m* néisc
> iascach múir.   TMIV,   pp. 62–63

Since rhythmic reiteration characterizes so much early Irish verse,
and since this reiteration is frequently regulated by strict repetition
of the incidence and number of stresses (both strong and weak),
there is a close relation between stress organization and syllable
count in the Old Irish verse line. This tendency may be enunciated
as follows: *the degree of reiteration in stress rhythm tends to determine
the regularity of syllable count in the Old Irish verse line.*
   Old Irish verse of lyric or shamanistic intent, and verse that
mimics the repetitious rhythm of work or dance or marching, tends
to be regular in rhythm and hence typically uniform in the syllabic
count of its verse line. Where verse is used for utility—in prayer,
in genealogies and in statements of law—the rhythm is typically
more varied and the syllable count more irregular doubtless because,
in such verse, matter takes precedence over form, and perhaps

also because such verse reflects a very early tradition, antecedent to the development of the *alliterative accentual* style and even of strongly accentual speech. And yet archaic utilitarian verse has the same basic rhythmic line as much other Old Irish verse.

This verse—in the cadential structure of its line, in the apportioning of its half-line lengths, and in its occasional use of initial and closing short lines that lack caesura—reveals structure whose most general analytic expressions are comparable to the basal verse lines of Vedic, Greek and Slavic, and hence require, for rationalization, the invocation of Indo-European archetypes. These archetypes are the structural fountainhead of Indo-European verse in both the languages (such as Greek and Sanskrit) that developed poetic rhythms from vowel quantity and pitch, and the languages (such as Germanic and Celtic) that eventually developed poetic rhythms from accentual stress.

Without regard to the incidence of strong and weak stresses but only as to their normative number before and after normative caesura, the Old Irish archetypal verse lines may be represented as follows: (WIEM, pp. 212–46 [especially pp. 245–46])

Old Irish long line:	(x) x x x x x x (x)
Old Irish short line	
with caesura:	(x) x x x x (x)
without caesura:	(x) x x x (x)

The rise of accentual speech among the Celts and Germans, and the attendant development of an *alliterative accentual* verse style, with its processions of paired stresses, advanced the following stress pattern as preeminently the basic heroic line of Germanic verse, and as one of the basic lines of Celtic epic verse:[9]

$$- - x - - - - x - - \, || \, - - x - - - - x - -$$

Hýge sceal be héardra, héorte be cénre
Éo Róssa, róth rúirech

This stress pattern, which prevailed in Germanic heroic verse for millennia, was by no means exclusively the pattern of the Celtic heroic verse line. In the Welsh epic *Y Gododdin*, an Indo-European long line persisted whose parts are three, a line also evident in some Old Irish survivals:

(x) x x x   (x) x x x (x)   x x x (x)

ne llewes/ef vedgwyn/vei noethyd.

e neges/ef or drachwres/drenghidyd.

tut vwlch hir/ech e dir/ae dreuyd.   CA,   p. 5[10]

fo cen breth/breithemun brighach/nimglinde   3/5/3
a teit for fuighell/airgech rechtuid/rigoilech   5/4/3
atabonar/trebh ar teidhmnech/turranach   4/4/3

WIEM,   p. 242

(It will be seen in our discussion of verse paragraph and stanza
that triadic stanzas appear to exfoliate from the Welsh epic long
line of three parts.)   Further, in *Y Gododdin,* in the typical line
with caesura the first part tends to be longer than the second—
usually by one syllable, sometimes by two and infrequently by three:

(x) x x x x x x x x (x)

dygymyrrws eu hoet/eu hanyanawr.   6/4
med evynt melyn/melys maglawr.   5/4

coch eu cledyuawr/na phurawr   5/3   CA,   p. 4

A less common line in *Y Gododdin* is the epic line par excellence
of early Old French epic, the decasyllabic line with caesura after
the fourth syllable:

x x x x   x x x x x x

ruthyr eryr/en *ebyr* pan llithywyt.

gwell a wnaeth/e aruaeth ny gilywyt.

hyder gymhell/ar vreithel vanawyt.   CA,   p. 2

Rodlanz at mis/l'olifant a sa boche   BCR,   l. 814

Rodlanz est proz/et Oliviers est sages   BCR,   l. 1093

Halt sont li pui/e li val tenebros   BCR,   l. 1753

This line, which is also the line of Slavic epic, recalls the archaic
Greek paroemiac and hence leads again to Indo-European archetypes.

Musical Regulation and the Verse Foot

The coincidence of lyricism and rhythmic regulation, noted above (p. 12), suggests the formative influence of music, as well as of mood. Music promotes regularity of the purely rhythmic and formal elements of associated verse.

That Celtic music was performed coincidently with Celtic poetry is evidenced by metrical tracts, ancient laws, common musico-poetic terminology and certain characteristics common to Celtic music and early Celtic verse. Musicians and bards attended the *filid* when these learned poets made their formal visitations among the great clan centres of Ireland. The regulative influence of music must have especially influenced the contours of folk poetry since the folk minstrels or *bards* (but not the *filid*) were at once poets and musical performers.

One effect of music on associated verse would be the tendency of the musical phrase to enforce its stress or beat structure on lyrics written to the music, so that consecutive stanzas would tend to have the same disposition of stresses per verse line. Whenever a poet composed a paragraph or two of lyric verse before he (or his musicians) conceived a suitable melody for the lyric, the rhythm of the poetry would inspire the rhythm of the melody; but the melody, once devised, would tend to unify the rhythm of all verse paragraphs (or stanzas) subsequently conceived.

A second effect of music on associated verse would be to conform the duration and intensity of each vocal stress (whether strong or weak) with the duration and stress of the musical beat. Although musical beat or rhythm likely takes initial form from the dynamics of speech, once musical form has concretized, its own unique dynamics can operate reflexively on the speech that initially inspired it. The influence of Celtic song on associated verse would be to lighten the intensity of strong vocal stresses, and to lengthen the duration of weak stresses. The strongly accentual early Irish and early Welsh speech would be modulated, when sung, to a rhythm that would supply the weaker speech stresses with time values or durations tangibly longer than those given the same stresses in dry speech.

A third effect of music on associated verse would be to overcome diaeresis and catalexis within the verse line or within the musical phrase and, on the other hand, to enforce a pause at the end of the phrase. This is because the dynamics of musical development provides for a continuity of sound and rhythm throughout the musical phrase, and would thus tend to require a comparable continuity of poetic expression, as to both sense and speech stress.

To recapitulate: bardic verse, because of the regulative influence of music, would tend to be (1) regular in the stress or syllable count of its lines, (2) stanzaic in form, (3) relatively free of diaeresis within the verse line, (4) relatively regular in cadence and line-end catalexis, and (5) relatively lighter in the intensity of its strong stresses, and longer in the duration of its weak stresses. Bardic verse in fact reflects these tendencies strikingly.

Until recently, one could not verify in detail the similarities of rhythmic and formal development disclosed in early Celtic poetry and music, because no Celtic music which was incontestably antique was known. The use of common terms, in both Welsh and Irish, for poetic and musical forms was of course suggestive. In early Welsh, *gosteg, caniad* and *caniad marwnad* are terms for specific kinds of verse and also for specific kinds of music. But the nature of this music remained unknown, despite its existence in considerable quantity. Decipherment and analysis of the previously baffling tablature that preserves the music now permits of close comparison between the rhythms of its phrases and the rhythms of Old Irish and Old Welsh verse lines.[11]

The beats or stresses of the early poetic and the early musical lines correlate very closely. The melodic phrases of early Celtic harp music are composed of beats or stresses whose numbers range from two to eleven per phrase, with a preponderance in certain compositions of phrases containing stresses from five to nine. The analytic representation of the archetypal Old Irish verse lines given above (pp. 13-14) adequately represents also the normative phrases of the early harp music. The parallels between the number and arrangement of stresses in the line of early Celtic verse and in the phrase of early Celtic harp music are indicative of a close relation, especially as this Celtic musical phrase is distinguished by unique particulars from the phrases of other European music.

It seems likely that Celtic song-form evolved from the same rhythm as pervades early Celtic verse. This basic rhythm finds its musical expression in triplet formations (*morfine, caraimse, amra, issed, adfet*):

Just as pairs of balanced or contrasted words make up the measure in *word foot* rhythm, so pairs of balanced or contrasted rhythmical units make up the rudimentary musical motif or section:

Similarly, just as the dimeter grows out of a systematic pairing of measures, so the musical section becomes a double section or 'phrase':

The musical 'period' or double phrase is the analogue of the long verse made up of two dimeters:

The couplet of long verses or the quatrain of short verses is the formal equivalent of the double period or the simple two-part song form:

In brief, the strong evidence of interrelation between Celtic music and verse, including mutual development from common rhythmic elements, confirms the thesis that music early assisted in the regulation of Old Celtic verse rhythm. This regulatory influence of music on the rhythm and form of verse is not a peculiarly Celtic phenomenon. Chinese verse by the fifth century BC, although its religious chants show many irregular lines, had Classic songs, which were lyrics in regular stanzas with lines of uniform dimensions, that is, quatrains with four stresses (*word feet*) per line. (EPP, p. 118) In Fiji verse, words are arbitrarily lengthened to match the musical line. (QFC, p. 14) Even in English, an otherwise silent final syllable may be given stress when sung: gatheréd, pardonéd.

So far as rhythm is concerned, the end result of the influence of Celtic song on its attendant lyrics would be the emergence of a *verse foot* that recognized no distinction of trochee or iamb, dactyl or anapaest, but rather only a stress complex of strong and weak, or weak and strong. This verse foot would freely admit of feet whose stress structures could be termed iambic, trochaic, dactylic and anapaestic. Such a rhythmic concept is analogous to a common usage in Prakrit poetry, whereby only the total quantity of each foot is taken into account, each short syllable being one matra and each long syllable being two. (EPP, p. 394)

The Celtic verse foot, evolving obviously from musical regulation, occurs alike in the Old Irish and the finest Hiberno-Latin lyrics and hymns. This foot accommodates words of varied stress structure, and hence permits of a poetry whose accentual rhythms avoid repetitiousness or jingling. By its nature, the Celtic verse foot offers the potential of rhythmic freedom, inasmuch as this foot consists of strong and weak stresses in various sequences or combinations: the strong stress may precede or follow the weak; and the foot may contain more than one strong and more than one weak stress. For this reason, Celtic verse rhythms have somewhat the freedom of speech rhythms.[12]

Each Celtic verse foot within a passage will tend to be roughly the same in duration, as in successive bars of a musical measure or phrase; but this approach to uniformity of verse-foot duration is the only predominating uniformity implicit in the foot itself. The continuing influence of archaic rhythms and traditional forms tended to perpetuate a Celtic rhythmic style, whose feeling transcended the distinctions drawn here among levels of rhythmic sophistication. In consequence, Celtic rhythm is recognizable as such whether its embodiment is the *word foot*, the *word measure* or the Celtic verse foot. Once aware of the quite special verse foot of Old Irish and Hiberno-Latin poetry, the student has no difficulty in scansion; and the concept of a poetry that is both rhythmless and at the same time highly regulated in the accentual rhythm of its verse-ends can be set aside.

A basic problem preventing awareness of the character of early Celtic (and also early Italic and Germanic) verse rhythm has been the attempt, from the outset of Celtic studies, to interpret bi-accentual rhythmic phenomena in terms of a uno-accentual metric that derives ultimately from the quantitative measures of classical Greece. The bi-accentual stress of many early Celtic and Italic tri-syllabic words is the rock on which classical prosodists have foundered: *triumpe, cutulsa, ollechtach, Fomoire, iuuate, semunis, alternei*. Early Latin ritual, popular Latin in the Saturnian rhythms, early Hiberno-Latin, Old Irish and Welsh verse—none of these poetries can be made to fit a uno-accentual straitjacket; but, once the incidence of bi-accentual *word feet* and *word measures* is recognized, the consistency and the systematic character of bi-accentual rhythm in early Celtic and Italic verse become perfectly apparent.

The total duration of the double stress in such words as *cutulsa, ollechtach, triumpe, semunis* is substantially the same as the duration of the single stress in such words as *Mars, Goidel, pleoris, blaith*.

The first stress of a double stress is shorter in duration than the
second. In actual speech, an indefinite number of variations would
be verifiable in the relative duration of the two adjoining stresses.
For purposes of metrical scansion or of musical setting, the second
stress of the pair could be assigned a duration twice that of the
first:

The duration of the unstressed final syllable(s) would vary substantially in speech. In recitation, and especially in a musical
setting, the duration of the unstressed syllable(s) would be modi-
fied to approach a rough uniformity in the total duration of the
unitary foot. Once a verse foot is recognized, its inherent propensities toward uniformity of duration impose a measure on the
verse that departs from the rhythms of dry speech and approaches
the generalized rhythms of musical utterance; and this propensity
is heightened by the practice of rendering verse in song, or to
musical accompaniments.

A few examples, with musical scoring to aid scansion, will suffice
to illustrate the characteristics of early Irish verse-foot rhythm,
which may be schematized as follows:

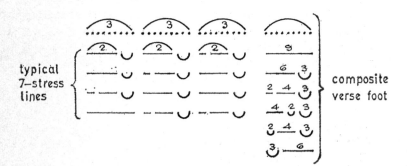

These musical indications of relative duration are not to be taken either as absolutes or as precise mensuration. Further, if they suggest likely musical settings, it must be remembered that the actual wedding of verse and music often involves a considerable accommodation of poetic to musical rhythm—sometimes to the extent of destroying the rhythmic intention of the poetry. Some musicians would tend to impose a 6/8 rhythm on *Brigit be bithmaith*; and a 9/8, on *Munther Benchuir beata*:

2

Paragraph and Stanza

Though the articulation of vocal stress constitutes basic rhythm in early Celtic verse, form in this verse evolves from the interplay of stress and grammatical patterns. Specific Celtic verse forms emerge from particular usages and emphases in the repetition, complemental variation and apposition of interrelated grammatical and stress patterns.

Incremental repetition, the refrain and the sequencing of paired stresses are basic devices in the formal organization of repetitive, variational, and appositional elements. Their occurrence in the earliest Welsh and Irish verse makes it possible to relate the various classes of stanzaic form in Celtic verse to indigenous antecedents.

Sequencing of Paired Stresses

The sequencing of paired stresses develops verse paragraphs of indeterminate length and also (under certain conditions, such as grammatical symmetry or musical regulation) stanzas of set form, typically but not invariably four lines long. In poems constructed by sequencing paired stresses, the poem progresses by pairs of words or word clusters whose stress structure provides pairs of rhythmic units, and these units may be in turn paired, and the double-units may be paired again. From such pairing, the couplet and the quatrain, sestet, octet, etc. can emerge. On the other hand, the progress of coupled pairs can continue indefinitely within the paragraph (as in *Eo Rossa*, p. 3, above).

Stanzas would occasionally occur in a verse of paired stresses merely in reflection of sporadically recurring grammatical symmetries; however, the appearance of consecutive stanzas identical in stress but not in grammatical structure would seem to betoken conscious intent. Even so, the strophe of indeterminate length will not give way all of a piece to stanzaic form; rather, couplets, triads, quatrains, etc. will appear sporadically before systematically.

After opening with a verse paragraph composed of four quatrains and two couplets, the early Welsh epic *Y Gododdin* follows with fifteen monorime paragraphs. The seventeenth paragraph includes five couplets and four quatrains. The eighteenth paragraph opens with three quatrains; then follow a triad and a nine-line monorime.

17. Anawr gynhoruan
    huan arwyran.
    gwledic gwd gyfgein
    nef enys brydein.
    garw ryt rac rynn;
    aes e lwrw budyn.
    bual oed arwynn
    eg kynted eidyn.
    e rihyd ryodres.
    e ved medwawt
    yuei win gwirawt.
    oed eruit uedel;
    yuei win gouel.
    a erueid en arued;
    aer gennin vedel.
    Aer adan glaer.
    kenyn keuit aer.
    Aer seirchyawc
    aer edenawc.
    nyt oed diryf y ysgwyt
    gan waywawr plymnwyt.
    kwydyn gyuoedyon;
    eg cat blymnwyt.
    diessic e dias;
    divevyl as talas.
    hudit e wyllyas.
    kyn bu clawr glas
    bed gwruelling vreisc. CA, p. 7

18. Teithi etmygant
    tri llwry nouant.
    pymwnt a phymcant.
    trychwn a thrychant.
    tri si chatvarchawc;
    eidyn eu ruchawc.
    tri llu llurugawc;

> tri eur deyrn dorchawc.
> tri marchawc dywal;
> tri chat gyhaual.
> tri chysneit kysnar;
> chwerw fysgynt esgar.
> tri en drin en drwm.
> llew lledynt blwm;
> eur e gat gyngrwn.
> tri theyrn maon;
> a dyvu o vrython.
> kynri a chenon.
> kynrein o aeron.
> gogyuerchi ynhon
> deivyr diuerogyon.
> a dyvu o vrython
> wr well no chynon
> sarff seri alon. CA, p. 8

A parallel with early Welsh epic, from a ruder level of artistry, is presented by certain traditional Fiji poems, whose preponderantly monorime paragraphs may be varied by sporadic change in rime. In some instances, these rime changes, by their frequency and regularity, approach stanzaic form. (QFC, pp. 15–16, 106, 223)

Couplets and quatrains will not necessarily be all of a kind in the first phase of their recognition as formal units. A poem in quatrains will not necessarily employ a continuous succession of quatrains identical in structure and ornament. Their rhythm will tend to be more uniform than their verse-ends, and their verse-ends will not necessarily be ornamented by rime or its variants (assonance and consonance). These aspects of stanzaic development are represented among the surviving specimens of Old Irish verse. In *Coimdiu caid cumachtach* (p. 10), only the last lines of the two stanzas rime. Rimeless quatrains survive: *Mal adrualaid* (p. 9), *Mair drecain* (p. 10), *Or os grein* (p. 9), *Nimthang tadg* (p. 10); and the following, attributed to the pagan poet-king *Lugair lanfili*:

> Doss dāile/dāl Temro,
> toccad cāin/cōemnae cōecat blīadnae.

Ba barr fīne/fīal caur Cathāir Mār:
mairgg Elcgae!/addaimet a lecht Lūaigne.

MAID II, p. 15

Poems also survive whose successive stanzas exhibit varying structural patterns at the verse-ends. Thus, the first stanza of *Atchiu fer find firfes chless* (p. 37 below) is common *debide*; but succeeding stanzas vary in the treatment of riming verse-ends:

> Fail secht gemma láth ṅ-gaile
> ar lar a dá imcaisne,
> fail fuidrech for a rinne,
> fail lǽind deirg drolaig imme.
>
> Ro fail gnúis is grátam dó,
> dober mod don banchuireo,
> gilla óc is delbdu dath
> tadbait delb drecoin don chath.
>
> Nocon fetar cóich in cú
> Culaind asa Murthemniu,
> acht ra fetar-sa tra imne
> bid forderg in sluag sa de.
>
> Cethri claidbíni cless n-án
> ra fail cechtar a da lám,
> condricfa a n-imbirt for slúag,
> isaingním ris téit cech n-ai úad.   TBC, p. 35

The survival of Old Irish stanzaic verse in forms that seem transitional does not necessarily mean that such forms were short-lived or that their use was no earlier than the date of surviving specimens. Evidence is abundant that Old Irish poets tended towards the archaic—to use forms that, on a chronological or analytic schema, would appear to have been transitional or obsolete. Further, in some of the most highly ornate and complex Old Irish and Hiberno-Latin verse, a slight but orderly variation in stanzaic structure was apparently cultivated on aesthetic grounds, to intensify the inter-stanzaic correspondences. Such verse cannot be considered transitional in the sense of a sporadic and inadequate groping toward uniformity; rather, its regular irregularity demonstrates a complex and subtle versecraft whose richness of effect is not attainable through the identical repetition of a single stanzaic pattern. This versecraft is manifest in both Old Irish and Hiberno-Latin verse (as is shown in Part II, below).

Virtuosity in variation among stanzaic patterns within a single poem can be demonstrated aptly in genealogical verse. Although such verse would intrinsically incline toward paragraphs, stanzas or couplets of roughly equal dimensions (so as to afford each ancestor equal recognition), Old Irish genealogical verse avoided, in some instances, the regularity of Biblical *begats* in favour of an artistic adaptation of rhythm and form to the individual aspects of specific ancestors. Thus early genealogies that appear, from one view, as merely irregular in stanzaic structure may be better viewed as a series of quatrains deliberately distinctive in rhythm and form, each suited to a traditional epithet for the particular person.

Genealogical verse was the prerogative of the *filid*, who served the clan leaders. It would not have been sung to folk melody, as with the verse of the *bards*: rather, it would have been chanted or declaimed, with such musical accompaniment as would support a recitative. Genealogical verse, being utilitarian and hence plastic in its accommodation of subject matter, necessarily governed the form of any music that may have attended its recitation—a circumstance that would account for the freedom of its rhythms, and for the frequency of structural change in its quatrains.

In accommodating genealogical subject matter, poets (and these the most professional) certainly utilized all the modes of Old Irish rhythm: the *word foot*, the *word measure* and the Celtic verse foot. The quatrains that exemplify this rhythmic variety also verify the use of specific quatrain forms, centuries before the date of their description in the Old Irish metrical tracts.

Numerical Analogues

The efficacy of paired stresses in generating poetic and musical form will be granted, in view of our discussion on this point. This efficacy would seem to reside at least partially in the operation, conscious or unconscious, of a concern with or feeling for number, and specifically the binary number series—basic arithmetical and geometrical progressions—2, 4, 6, 8, 10 etc.; and 2, 4, 8, 16 etc.

If such a concern with number in application to poetic form had become conscious among learned Celts one would nevertheless assume that the operation of numerical measure, in the earliest Celtic, Italic and Germanic verse, originated in the unconscious and hence represented initially a *natural* process, as in the music of some birds and insects whose patterns of expression will disclose numerical analogues.

There would be reason to suspect that numerical analogues with poetic rhythm and form became eventually a matter of conscious intellection among the learned pagan Celts, if only because the community of ideas between Celts and Pythagoreans—to whom number was the basis of all things—was so persistently noticed by antique Greek scholarship.[13] The facts of early Celtic artistic development permit us more than suspicions.

Pagan Celtic design on stone and metal, and its early application to Christian manuscript decoration, discloses an incredibly clever use of the compasses in the analysis and reintegration of ornamental motifs, and a conscious interplay of triadic and quadrangular elements. Celtic memorial crosses offer striking analogues to antique Greek proportion in addition to Christian number-symbolism.[14] The system of musical analysis and composition underlying classical Celtic harp music rests entirely on binary and tertiary numerical analogues—the harmonies alternate to binary measures, the chords (however dissonant their position) are built of thirds, the rhythms are reducible to duple and triple beat units, and the melodic phrases are sums of the rhythmic units (as Celtic verse lines have been shown to be—pp. 2-21 above).[15]

Whereas the use of paired stresses as structural units has analogies with binary number series, the use of triadic forms has analogies with tertiary numbers. The combination of triadic repetition with the quatrain stanza can be regarded as strictly analogous to the early—and pagan—Celtic accommodation of triadic and quadrangular motifs in design.

Triadic Form: Iteration and Refrain

The germ of triadic form is the threefold iteration of a word or phrase. Such iteration takes us far back in time for its origins, and to primitive levels of artistic technique for examples.

Two whole orders of triadic forms must have underlain the development of the triad as it appears in the earliest Celtic documentation. Though primitive substrata have left broad traces in Celtic verse, for an adequate notion of the substrata one must turn to verse composed by the direct repetition of words, phrases, statements and grammatical formulae; that is, to the chants of primitive religion—the hymns of the Arval Brethren, of the early Christians, of the American negro, etc.

Primitive verse, from the nursery rhyme to the negro spiritual, employs in one of its modes a stanza composed of a thrice-stated line, followed by a fourth line that may or may not be a refrain:

> Lit'l Boy, how old are you?
> Lit'l Boy, how old are you?
> Lit'l Boy, how old are you?
> Sir, I'm only twelve years old.

> —negro spiritual

The three-line iteration of a grammatical, rhythmic or aural element presents a verbal pattern whose origin must be sought ultimately in primitive psychology. Threefold iterations are common in the verse of cultures widely disparate in time and place; the triadic or triangular motif is a nearly universal element in the arts, and it occurs often in nature. Primitive religious expression employs it. The triad made up of a triple utterance we designate the prototriad, for from it issues a family of forms, when to it are conjoined refrains and incremental variation.

A forms array can be reconstructed for primitive substrata of triadic verse. Most species of the array are available: gaps in the array can be filled by regarding the formal principles that underlie species at hand.

The threefold iteration of a single word or statement is the most elementary level of triadic utterance. It is evidenced in early Christian liturgy:

> Kyrie eleison
> Kyrie eleison
> Kyrie eleison

An equally elementary form of variation occurs in the second triad of this liturgical plea—the same verb, with a change in substantive:

> Christe eleison
> Christe eleison
> Christe eleison

In the early Italic prayer of the Arval Brethren, the threefold iterations involve change in the entire substance of successive statements:

> Enos Lases iuuate. (*thrice*)
> Neue lue rue Marmar sins incurrere in pleores. (*thrice*)
> Satur fu, fere Mars: limen sali, sta berber. (*thrice*)
> Semunis alternei aduocapit conctos. (*thrice*)
> Enos Marmar iuuato. (*thrice*)
> Triumpe, triumpe, triumpe, triumpe, triumpe! DLHR, p. 58

The same order or substratum of verse reveals also a formal concept whereby the first line or unit of the threefold iteration changes, and the second and third recur. The first line may change entirely, or only incrementally:

> Wasn't it a pity and a shame!
> And He never said a mumberlin' word,
> Oh, not a word, not a word, not a word.
>
> They nailed Him to the tree,
> And He never said, etc.
>
> —negro spiritual

The second line, or the third, may carry the change, with the other two lines recurring; and the change may be either entire or incremental:

> Yn Aber Cuawc yt ganant gogeu
> Ar gangheu blodeuawc.
> Coc lauar, canet yrawc.

> Yn Aber Cuawc yt ganant gogeu
> Ar gangheu blodeuawc.
> Gwae glaf a'e clyw yn vodawc. CLH, p. 23

Triadic variation at the elementary level includes also a formal procedure antithetical to the one just indicated: one line (first, second or third) recurs; the other two lines change, whether entirely or only incrementally:

> Y gelein ueinwenn a oloir hediw
> Dan weryt ac arwyd.
> Gwae vy llaw llad vy arglwyd. CLH, p. 14

> Y gelein veinwen a oloir hediw
> A dan brid a mein glas.
> Gwae vy llaw llam ry'm gallas. CLH, p. 15

> Stauell Gyndylan ys tywyll heno,
> Heb dan, heb wely;
> Wylaf wers tawaf wedy.

> Stauell Gyndylan ys tywyll heno,
> Heb dan, heb gannwyll;
> Namyn Duw, pwy a'm dyry pwyll? CLH, p. 35

> The hall of Cynddylan is dark to-night,
> Without fire, without bed;
> I will weep a while, I will be silent after.

> The hall of Cynddylan is dark to-night,
> Without fire, without candle;
> Except God, who will give me sanity?[16]

The fourteen elemental variants of the simplest triadic form of utterance are multiplied by the use of an additional line as refrain, producing a triadic quatrain. Threefold iterations, changing throughout successive stanzas in any of the fourteen ways indicated above, may be unified by the recurrence of a first, second, third or fourth line as refrain:

Were you there when they crucified my Lord?
Were you there when they crucified my Lord?
Oh, sometimes it causes me to tremble, tremble, tremble,
Were you there when they crucified my Lord?

Were you there when they pierced Him in the side?
      etc., etc.

Were you there when they laid Him in the tomb?
      etc., etc.

—negro spiritual

Antithetically, the new matter of the stanza may be contained in a single line (first, second, third or fourth) and the remaining three lines will recur throughout as a triadic refrain:

One mile he completed
Thick was the darkness, light was there none
In this dusk he can see not
What lies behind him

Two miles he completed
Thick was the darkness, etc.

Three miles he completed
Thick was the darkness, etc. GL, p. 43

The triad early appeared at a higher level of complexity or abstraction than that represented by threefold iterations. At this higher level the triad is one complete statement in three units or periods, capable of the same formal variation as the elemental triad, by use of incremental repetition and the refrain. The triad that is one tripartite statement generalizes form by making it independent of any specific statement. The essence of triadic form at this level is grammatical structure. It is this structure with whose pattern the matter of successive triads will seek to conform.

The verse of Babylonia and ancient Egypt (before 2000 BC) discloses triads of this higher level, in which the three-period statement is combined in successive triads with incremental repetition and refrains. The following series of triads appears in the old Babylonian version of the Gilgamesh epic (obviously anticipating the Biblical Flood story):

> Instead of thy rousing a stormflood,
> A lion could have risen up
> And diminished mankind;
> Instead of thy rousing a stormflood,
> A wolf could have risen up
> And diminished mankind;
> Instead of thy rousing a stormflood,
> Famine could have come
> And stricken down the land;
> Instead of thy rousing a stormflood,
> The god of pestilence could have risen
> And stricken down the land. GL, p. 68

Similar to the Babylonian triads, and quite close in feeling to some early Welsh verse written almost three millennia later, the following triads appear in the Egyptian *Dialogue of the Despairing Man with his Soul:*

> Death is before me today
> Like health for the invalid
> Like going out after an illness
> Death is before me today
> Like the odor of myrrh
> Like sitting under the sail on a windy day
> Death is before me today
> Like the desire of a man to see his home again
> After numberless years of captivity. EPP, p. 213

Early Celtic verse generalizes triadic form still further by formalizing the incidence of its ornament. Through the use of incremental repetition and refrains, Celtic triads retain the same capability of structural variation as appears in more primitive substrata. At the same time, a demanding pattern of verse ornament must be met recurrently from stanza to stanza, a pattern independent of both meaning and grammatical structure (as appears, for example, in the triads quoted from *Clef Abercuawg* and *Celain Urien*).

From Paragraph to Stanza

The triadic quatrain led ultimately to the stanza type termed *ochtfochlach* in early Irish metrical tracts. One may attend the birth, as it were, of such stanzas. They emerge sporadically from the body of the monorime verse paragraph in the oldest surviving Welsh verse, the epic lay *Y Gododdin;* and they appear also systematically throughout entire lyrics both within this epic and in separate poems:

Gwr a aeth gatraeth gan dyd.
ne llewes ef vedgwyn vei noethyd.
bu truan gyuatcan gyvluyd.
e neges ef or drachwres drenghidyd.
  ny chryssyws gatraeth
  mawr mor ehelaeth
    e aruaeth uch arwyt.
  ny bu mor gyffor
  o eidyn ysgor
    a esgarei oswyd
tut vwlch hir ech e dir ae dreuyd.
ef lladei saesson seithuet dyd.
perheit y wrhyt en wrvyd
ae govein gan e gein gyweithyd.
pan dyvu dutvwlch dut nerthyd.
oed gwaetlan gwyaluan vab kilyd. CA, p. 5

Eveis y win a med e mordei.
  mawr meint e vehyr
  ygkyuaruot gwyr.
    bwyt e eryr erysmygei.
  pan gryssyei gydywal kyfdwyreei.
  awr gan wyrd wawr kyui dodei.
aessawr dellt anibellt a adawei.
  pareu rynn rwygyat
  dygymynei. e gat
    blaen bragat briwei
mab syvno; sywyedyd ae gwydyei.
  a werthws e eneit
  er wyneb grybwyllyeit;
    a llavyn lliveit lladei.
lledessit ac athrwys ac affrei;
er amot aruot aruaethei.
  ermygei galaned
  o wyr gwychyr gwned
    em blaen gwyned gwanei. CA, pp. 8–9

Guir gormant aethant cennin
gwinweith a medweith oedyn
   o ancwyn mynyđauc
anthuim cim mruinauc
   o goll gur gunet rin
mal taran[aur]
nem tarhei scuytaur
   rac rynnaud eithinin.   CA,   p. 18

  O winveith a medweith
dygodolyn. gwnlleith
   mam hwrreith eidol enyal.
ermygei rac vre
rac bronn budugre
   bre/ein dwyre wybyr ysgynnyal.
kynrein en kwydaw
val glas heit arnaw;
   heb gilyaw gyhaual.
synnwyr ystwyr ystemel;
y ar weillyon gwebyl
   ac ardemyl gledyual.
blaen ancwyn anhun
hediw an dihun;
   mam reidun rwyf trydar.   CA,   p. 27

Aryf angkynnull
angkyman dull; twryf en agwed.
e rac meuwed.
e rac mawrwed. e rac mar yed.
pan ystyern gwern.
e am gamgyrn. e am gamgled.
e uoli [llawr]
ri; a lluawr peithliw racwed.
yd i gweles;
ar hual tres tardei galled.   CA,   p. 50

But of course it is unlikely that these particular instances of emergent stanza constitute the first examples merely because *Y Gododdin* is old. The compositional technique of *Y Gododdin* may well be a millennium older than the poem itself. One must reiterate what is true of Celtic art generally: forms seemingly

transitional are rarely transitory. Thus, the Welsh epic verse line
from which triadic stanzas emerge, marking its tripartite divisions
with their end-rimes, in fact descends directly from the Indo-
European long line.

The triadic quatrain, in its matured form, transcends both
incremental repetition and the terminal refrain by formalizing
the ornament or sound-harmony of the verse line. Intralinear
ornament and end-rime generalize the recurrent sound provided
originally by incremental repetition and refrains:

> Rat fíat láich rat láma,
> no co raga ar dála,
> sréin *ocus* eich ána
> ra bhertar rit láim.
> A Fir-d*iad* i*n*n ága,
> dáig isat duni dána,
> dam-sa bat fer gráda,
> sech cách gan nach cáin.
>
> Ni rag-sa gan rátha
> do chluchi na n-átha,
> meraid collá ṁ-brátha,
> go bruth is co m-bríg.
> Noco géb, ge ésti,
> ge ra beth dom résci,
> gan gréin ocus ésci
> la muir ocus tír.   TBC,   p. 447

The emergence of stanza from the verse paragraph of indeterminate
length follows more than one path.

In the Welsh *Marwnad Cynddylan*, the final two lines recur as
an incrementally repetitive refrain for the first eight paragraphs.
In this poem, all paragraphs after the first (of which a fragment
survives) begin with incrementally repetitive lines, and the repetition
extends to lines beyond the first. A similar use of incremental
repetition and the refrain occurs in the Old French epic, *Voyage de
Charlemagne.* (TPPD) These Old Welsh and Old French epic lays
use a verse paragraph whose each line ends in monorime (Old
Welsh) or in a common assonance (Old French). (Such paragraphs
are but a step short of monorime stanzas whose refrains provide a
second rime.)

Mawredd gyminedd a feddyliais
Myned i Fenai, cyn ni'm bai fais.
Carafi a'm enneirch o dir Cemais,
Gwerling Dogfeiling Cadelling trais.
Ef cwynif oni fwyf i'm derw llednais,
O leas Cynddylan, colled anofais.

Mawredd gyminedd, i feddyliaw
Myned i Fenai, cyn ni'm bai naw!
Carafi a'm enneirch o Aberffraw,
Gwerling Dogfeiling Cadelling ffaw.
Ef cwynif oni fwyf i'm derwin taw,
O leas Cynddylan, a'i luyddaw.

Mawredd gyminedd, gwin waredawg,
Wyf colledig wen, hen hiraethawg.
Collais pan amwyth alaf Pennawg
Gwr dewr diachar diarbedawg.
Cyrchai drais tra Thren, tu trahawg,
Ef cwynif oni fwyf yn ddaear fodawg,
O leas Cynddylan, clod Caradawg.   CLH,   pp. 50–51

The couplet can emerge through the truncation of monorime
stanzas or paragraphs and, equally obviously, through the orna-
menting of lines whose symmetry derives from the repetition of
grammatical formulae, from the sequencing of paired stresses,
or from both:

Trycant eurdorchauc
gwnedgar guacnauc
trychan trahaavc
kyuun kyuarvavc
trychan meirch godrud
a gryssyws ganthud
trychwn a thrychant
tru nyt atcorsant.   CA,   p. 45

Such formulae can involve simply the repetition of a pair of riming
lines at the beginning of successive monorime paragraphs. These
initial pairs become obvious couplets when used to introduce

consecutive paragraphs that otherwise change in end-rime. Such
couplets characterize the Irish lyric celebrating Cuchulain's fight
with Ferdiad, whose stanzas all begin:

> Cluchi cach gáine cach
> go roich Fer diad issin n-áth   TBC,   p. 595

An extended period of independent development underlies the
earliest documentation of the *debide* measures in Old Irish and
Welsh. Differences in usage between Wales and Ireland are, however,
consistent with the concept of a common prototype. The essence
of *debide* rime is its occurrence in a pair of lines in such manner
that the rime is accentual in one line of the couplet but not in the
other:

> Atchiu fer find firfes chless
> co lín chret ina chaemcnes,
> lond láith i n-airthiur a chind,
> oenach buada ina thilchind.   TBC,   p. 35

> Messe *ocus* Pangur Bán
> Cechtar nathar fria saindán
> Bíth a menmasam fri seilgg
> Mu menma céin im saincheirdd.

> Caraimse fos ferr cach clú
> Oc mu lebrán léir ingnu
> Ní foirmtech frimm Pangur Bán
> Caraid cesin a maccdán.   OSHI,   p. 52

> Gwell gwneif a thi
> ar wawt dy uoli.
> kynt y waet e lawr
> nogyt y neithyawr.
> kynt y vwyt y vrein
> noc y argyurein.
> ku kyueillt ewein.
> kwl y uot a dan vrein.
> marth ym p*a* vro
> llad vn mab marro.   CA,   p. 1

This particular kind of correspondence between ornament and accentual rhythm is another unique trait of Celtic versification. It can only have developed within a verse whose rhythm derives from stress. The *debide* measures, furthermore, appear to have been basically popular measures which because of their relatively easy requirements were particularly suited to balladic narrative. Between the earliest Welsh and Irish usage the common principle of *debide* rime is diversely applied. The Welsh and Irish usages of *cynghanedd* likewise differ in their *debide* measures. Their *debide* quatrains of paired couplets therefore take us back to Celtic prototypes of the pre-documentary period.

Paired couplets (rather than lines) are joined in most Old Irish stanzaic measures, and by rime that is accentual in the end word of both couplets. Less emphatic end-rime, in some stanzaic forms, may join the first and third lines; but in the preponderance of stanzaic forms, the end-rime in these lines finds its echo either internally to, or at the end of the second line of the couplet. Structurally, in the *debide* measures, end-rime joins paired lines; in the *rinnard* and *rannaigecht* measures, end-rime joins couplets, primarily; in the *ochtfochlach* measures, end-rime joins quatrains, primarily.[17] To the extent that the placement of ornament is compulsory at various set positions of the stanza, the stanzaic measures may be regarded as differing from one another in structure through the incidence of ornament. But this incidence, being related to stress rhythm, reinforces the principle that Celtic verse form derives from speech stress.

Emergence of amhrán

With the collapse of Irish society in the seventeenth century under the stress of imperialism, classical versecraft lost its socio-economic base, and a quite different verse rapidly emerged as the concern of both the popular and the professional poets. The professionals, so far as they survived in Ireland, became one with the submerged people. In Gaelic Scotland the professionals continued to enjoy an aristocratic patronage inasmuch as the traditional Highland social order, despite its reverses, continued to exist and to support its bards. Even so, the classical art declined in Scotland as in Ireland, and was gradually supplanted by a popular verse, termed *amhrán*.

Though this popular verse was not entirely new, it differed greatly from the classical in form and ornament. The phonetics of consonance was abandoned; only the vowel sounds mattered. Stressed syllables alone counted; the unstressed ceased to be closely regulated. End-rime was abandoned. Alliteration, though frequent, ceased to be compulsory. The verse lines within the stanza were unified by equality in the number of their stresses, and by correspondence in the quality of their stressed assonances. Was all this a *return*, comparable to the re-emergence of Anglo-Saxon alliterative verse in the Middle English period?

Verse of this 'new' kind was practised as a popular or folk art in early fourteenth-century Ireland, to judge from a denunciation of its practitioners. The *Liber Hymnorum* contains an early reference to *amhrán* accompanied by a harp, and an eleventh-century gloss on the word *amhrán*. Probably from an early period, the term denoted 'a song with regular stress rhythm and normally with frequent internal rime.' (MEIM, p. 24) Did this verse, which regards only stress and stressed assonance, extend to remote times? Its principles relate it to early Celtic-Italic-Teutonic styles.

The classical Old Irish measure termed *draignech* perhaps derived from early popular verse:

> Every stressed word, with the frequent exception of the first stressed word of each odd line, rimes with some word in another line, *aicill*, consonance, and alliteration being obligatory. The syllabic count of corresponding lines varies, however, from nine to as many as thirteen syllables. Perhaps in origin, therefore, it was a non-syllabic metre which was later adapted (very imperfectly) to the syllabic system. Each line of *draignech* has almost always four stressed words...
>
> MEIM, pp. 73–74

If a popular Celtic verse based on stressed assonance existed quite early in the historical period, we should not be totally surprised to find reflections of its style in Latin verse of the Celts or of the Celtic periphery. The following excerpt from a Mozarabic poem of the seventh century discloses a *word foot* rhythm of four stresses per line, with correspondence of the stressed assonances throughout the lines:

> Concèntos dùlces sonòras cònpares
> rèsonant in chòro diversòrum mòdulis[18]

The *Epitomes of Publius Virgilius Maro,* which appears to be a satire on rustic Latinity and specifically on such Celtic efforts as produced the *Hisperica Famina,* presents various specimens of verse in Latin that are obviously intended as ridicule. *Word foot* rhythm is prominent in these specimens, attributed to mythical poets and grammarians whose names are often of Celtic character. In at least one example, the *word foot* rhythm is ornamented by correspondence of stressed assonances, as with the Mozarabic specimen already noted:

Sòl màximus mùndi lùcifer
òmnia àëra inlùstrat pàriter   (VM,   p. 122)
—(attributed to a fictitious Gergesus)

From the evidence adduced, it would appear likely that beneath the notice of the professional poets a popular Celtic verse survived all along, from a period indefinitely remote until the seventeenth century when the surviving professionals took the verse in hand.

To summarize:

1 Early Celtic rhythm is based on speech stress.

2 The *word foot* and the *word measure* are primal Celtic rhythmic concepts.

3 Regulated or recurrent rhythm of the *word foot* and *word measure* produces, as a secondary consequence, a verse line whose syllable count is uniform.

4 The varieties of *word foot* and *word measure* rhythm produce all the variation in the syllabic count of verse lines that occurs in Celtic stanzaic forms.

5 The varieties of Celtic verse line correlate with Indo-European archetypes.

6 The Celtic verse foot evolves through musical regulation of the verse line.

7 Celtic verse form derives from the interplay of rhythmic and grammatical (or rhetorical) patterns.

8 Celtic verse forms are generated by the sequencing of paired stresses; by the triadic use of incremental repetition and refrains; and by the formal division of the epic long line.

- The Celtic couplet (and the quatrain, sestet, octet, etc.) evolves from the sequencing of paired stresses, coincidently with musical regulation and development.

- The Celtic triadic stanza evolves from primeval poetic substrata, utilizing incremental repetition and the refrain; and from the Welsh epic verse line of tripartite division.

9 The rhythm and form of Celtic verse derive from elements both indigenous and prehistoric.

- Celtic traits once ascribed to derivation from Christian Latin hymns derive rather from rhythm of the *word foot, word measure,* and Celtic verse foot; and from formal elements common to primitive or archaic verse of cultures separated by millennia of time and space.

- The cadential structure of Old Irish rimed verse occurs equally in Old Irish rimeless verse. The verse-ends are structurally and rhythmically identical, whether end-rime is present or absent. Old Irish stanzaic forms ornamented by end-rime survive also in rimeless equivalents. Triadic rimed stanzas emerge from the tripartite long line of Welsh epic.

- The terminology used for aspects of verse form (and ornament) in Old Irish metrical tracts is of indigenous origin. All the stanzaic forms in the Old Irish metrical treatises embody the rhythmic and formal elements of earlier Celtic verse.

10 A popular Celtic verse of stressed assonance appears to have existed from early times, but to have been ignored by the professional poets until the seventeenth century.

Part II : Ornament

3

Styles and Chronology

Old Irish verse is various in form and complex in ornament. Scholars have recognized two distinct styles, the *alliterative accentual* and the *riming stanzaic*. Considered relatively archaic, the *alliterative accentual* style is characterized by the use of alliteration between stressed sounds to ornament verse paragraphs of typically indeterminate length. Considered relatively 'new', the *riming stanzaic* style is characterized by the use of both alliteration and, even more, rime and its variants (consonance and assonance) to ornament set stanzas that are, for the most part, regular in stress and syllable count.

The 'new' style has been regarded by some scholars (but not all) as inspired by Irish exposure to Late Latin 'rimed prose' and to the Latin hymns introduced by such early evangelizers as St Patrick. Some scholars have attributed even the Old Irish *alliterative accentual* verse to Late Latin inspiration.

Whatever their pre-history may have been, all the styles of Old Irish verse flourished concurrently during the Old Irish period. They are fully developed in the earliest manuscripts and the earliest linguistic states. They exist combined in more than one major poem, including one of the oldest Christian poems that has survived in the vernacular. What is more, the distinct styles are three, not two.

A whole species of shamanistic verse—curses, satires, prophecies, divinations, pagan prayers, pagan hymns—combines non-stanzaic alliterative paragraphs as in the *alliterative accentual* verse with ornament, copiously applied, such as appears predominantly in the *riming stanzaic*. The shamanistic verse derives from druidical attempts to command and control the occult. It is the creation of the poet-druid as shaman—as medicine man, diviner, cult leader.

It combines in special ways the full panoply of the poet's craft for purposes of the utmost seriousness to a primitivistic society. The significance of this verse for theories of origin has been generally overlooked—its existence vitiates efforts to establish a chronology whereby the *riming stanzaic* verse, and its ornament, is held to be not merely 'new' but 'new' to the Old Irish period.

The alliteration in early Irish (and Teutonic) verse, but not in Late Latin, is accentual and reflects a relatively simple phonetic classification. Beyond alliteration, Irish (and also Welsh) verse ornament is uniquely phonetic: rime (and its variants) occurs between sounds that are aurally related in accordance with a passably scientific phonetic classification.

That Celtic alliteration observes a more rudimentary phonetics than all other Celtic ornament would seem to betoken its special prestige as the ornament of a verse style exalted in status and venerable in antecedents. The phonetics of Celtic rime (and its variants) being more advanced, the ornament based on this phonetics may reasonably be adjudged of more recent development than Celtic-Teutonic alliteration. But this development could have occurred at any time during the millennium between the close of the period of Celtic-Teutonic cultural intimacy on the continent (say 500 BC) and the first documentation of Old Irish verse (sometime in the sixth century AD). It is likely to have occurred well before the close of this millennium, because Celtic ornament utilizing the 'new' phonetics is a fully matured system by the time of its earliest documentation and further because this ornament is used copiously in Old Irish shamanistic verse, which certainly continued an early style.

Old Welsh verse survives in less variety than Old Irish; however, the same basic kinds occur—epic, lyric, shamanistic. The *monorime strophe* is primarily the vehicle of epic lay. The *riming stanza* is primarily the vehicle of lyric moods. Stylistic traits of the strophic and the stanzaic verse are often intermingled: complex and extended monorime strophes may contain stanzas; and stanzas of uniform dimension often employ monorime. Early Welsh shamanistic poems attributed to Taliesin express a transformism quite like that of the Old Irish hymn attributed to Amorgen.

The alliteration in Old Welsh verse reflects the same relatively simple phonetics as Old Irish alliteration. Old Welsh verse, however, rimes only sporadically in the Irish manner; for the most part,

Old Welsh rime occurs between identical sounds. One cannot find, in the oldest Welsh verse, that rime and its variants occur predominantly, as in Old Irish verse, between sounds that are aurally related (but not identical) in accordance with the passably scientific phonetic classification that underlies Old Irish rime; further, some of the so-called Irish rimes in early Welsh would be classed in Irish verse as assonance.

4

Rules

Alliteration in Old Irish is for the ear. Words normally alliterate between the initial sounds of their stressed syllables. Since Old Irish stress typically falls on the first syllable of words, alliteration occurs between stressed initial sounds.

The Irish words for alliteration, *úaim* and *comúaim*, signify 'stitching' or 'joining', and 'stitching together'. This joining or stitching is considered not to occur if a stressed sound separates otherwise alliterating sounds. The rules that follow apply to adjoining stresses, unless otherwise specified:

All vowels alliterate with one another. In eclipse, the radical initial sound alliterates. Thus, *n-* before vowels does not prevent alliteration; nor does *h*.

Generally in Old Irish verse, the consonants *c* and *g*, *t* and *d*, and *p* and *b* alliterate with each other. (In Middle Irish stanzaic verse, this alliteration of voiced and voiceless stops tends to occur only as a link between the close of one stanza and the beginning of the next.)

Of the double consonants beginning with *s*, the combinations of *s* with *l*, *n*, and *r* alliterate with one another; but the combinations of *s* with the voiced stops *b*, *g*, and *d* do not: the combination *sb* or *sg* or *sd* alliterates only with itself repeated.

A consonant alliterates (aside from the rules just given) with itself repeated or—except *f*, *s*, *p*—with its lenited form.

Greater freedom in the rules of alliteration prevails between stanzas, and between the lines of *alliterative accentual* verse, than within them. This freedom includes alliteration between stressed and unstressed sounds, between stressed sounds in the interior of compound words, between a sound interior to one word and the initial sound of another word, between eclipsing *n*- and radical initial *n*, between *f*, *p* or *s* and its lenited form, and even between unstressed words.

Although alliteration in the oldest Welsh verse usually occurs between identical consonants, there are sufficient instances of alliteration between phonetically related consonants to establish a similarity in principle between Irish and Welsh alliteration. Early Welsh practice is less stringent: alliteration occurs frequently between stressed and unstressed sounds, and stressed words may intervene between alliterating words. Not all features observable in early Irish practice can be documented in early Welsh; but this circumstance may be attributable, at least in part, to the paucity of early Welsh documentation.

Rime and its Variants

A close relation between ornament and stress marks both rime and alliteration. Consonance and assonance, however, occur independently of accent, though often coincidently with it. A special form of end-rime termed *debide* involves rime between accented and unaccented syllables.

Early Irish rime and its variants (consonance and assonance) are based on a phonetic classification of vowels and consonants which is a definite advance, scientifically, over the phonetics of early Celtic alliteration.[2] In early Irish verse the consonants are grouped for riming purposes as follows:

Voiceless stops: *p, c, t*

Voiced stops: *b, g, d*

Voiceless spirants: *f, ph, ch, th*

Voiced spirants and weak liquids: *bh, dh, gh, mh, l, n, r*

Strong liquids (double consonants); *ll, nn, ng, rr, mm, mb*

s

Perfect rime begins on the first stressed vowel, the corresponding stressed vowels are identical, all consonants subsequent to the first stressed vowel are of the same phonetic class and quality, and all long vowels in syllables after the first riming syllable are identical. Unstressed short vowels rime if of the same quality—*a, o, u* or *e, i*—when they follow a riming syllable. *Imperfect rime* differs from *perfect* in that corresponding consonants are the same as to quality but not as to class.

Perfect consonance occurs when corresponding vowels are of the same quantity, corresponding consonants or consonant groups are of the same class, and final consonants are of the same class and quality. *Imperfect consonance* does not require that consonants be of the same class.

There also occurs in Old Irish verse a sort of consonance very similar to one or two types of what in Welsh poetry is termed *cynghanedd*.[3] This ornament consists in parallelism, either simple or inverse, between the consecutive consonant sounds of adjoining words. This parallelism occurs independently of the number, value and arrangement of intervening vowel sounds. In Old Irish *cynghanedd*, the same phonetic groupings of consonants are recognized as in Old Irish rime. The following are some instances of this *cynghanedd*:

> sech *dru*ng*u dem*n*e*
> ro*roi*na *reu*n*n* (*Brigit be bithmaith*)
> di*u*d*erc*c *nd*er (*Amra Choluimb Chille*)
> Nida *dir de*rmait *da*la cach *rig ro*md*a*i (early genealogy)

Assonance is a correspondence of vowel sounds, without regard to consonants. End-assonance is often non-accentual. *Imperfect assonance* occurs between a monophthong and a diphthong containing, as one of its constituent elements, this monophthong:

> go n*oa*m   d*ia*n sossad   (*Amra Senain*)

Entrance-rime, internal rime, interlaced rime and inlaid (or heaped) rime are still other recognized forms of early Irish ornament. Entrance-rime consists in beginning successive or corresponding verse units with the same syllable or word, or with riming syllables or words. Internal rime occurs between the end word of one short verse line and a word in the interior of the next (or, rarely, between a word in the interior of one short verse line and the end word of the next). Interlaced rime occurs between words in the interior of consecutive or corresponding verse units. Inlaid rime occurs between words within the verse line.

The form of end-rime termed *debide* occurs between two paired
verse lines in which the rime word at the end of the first verse
line is one syllable shorter than the rime word at the end of the
second verse line.   In the shorter rime word, rime begins on the
accented vowel; in the longer rime word, the rime is typically
non-accentual, since it occurs on a syllable (or syllables) following
the first.   (*Debide* is illustrated in Part I, pp. 37-38).

The devices so far mentioned do not exhaust the variety of
Old Irish verse ornament.   Its complete rules, based on its practice,
have yet to be written.   For example, in some poems, a shorter
word rimes with the opening syllables or syllable of a longer word
rather than, as in *debide*, with the closing syllables (or syllable).
The more closely Old Irish verse is examined as to prosodic traits,
the less one credits certain generalizations long current.[4]

In Old Welsh verse, although it employs the same kinds of rime
as Old Irish (end, internal, inlaid, interlaced, etc.), the corresponding
sounds are usually identical rather than phonetically related.   Even
so, sufficient instances of phonetic (or generic) rime occur to establish
a similarity in principle between early Irish and Welsh rime.   Inasmuch as the final syllable of early Welsh words typically carried
the principal stress, end-rime was at one time normally accentual
in Old Welsh; but with the stress shift in various Welsh dialects
(at indefinite times) to the penultimate syllable, Welsh rime
eventually became only sporadically accentual.   Not all the distinctions observable in early Irish riming practice can be documented
in early Welsh—a circumstance possibly attributable to the fate of
libraries.   On the other hand, distinctively Welsh practices that
became compulsory in the ornament of various stanzaic forms by
the twelfth and thirteenth centuries already appear sporadically
in the strophes of Aneirin and the stanzas of Llywarch Hen.

In the Old Welsh epic *Y Gododdin*, a form of *cynghanedd* occurs
often, whereby two words internal to the verse line rime, and the
second of the two alliterates with the last word of the line:

> bu tru*an* **gy**uatc*an* **gy**vluyd.
> e neg*es* ef or **dr**achwr*es* **dr**enghidyd.
> tut vwlch h*ir* ech e **d**ir ae **d**reuyd.

This arrangement of rime and alliteration is systematically employed
in stanzaic verse of the Welsh court bards, six or seven centuries
after *Y Gododdin* was written.

The feeling for intralinear consonance is likewise strongly evident in the earliest Welsh verse. This consonance becomes systematically applied, centuries later, with the court bards: some of their stanzaic forms require that matching consonant sequences engage both halves of the verse line. But the disposition toward such ornament is already evident in *Y Gododdin*:

> gwr a aeth gatraeth gan dyd (g – r – th/g – r – th)
> perheit y wrhyt en wrvyd (rh – t/rh – t/r – d)
> oed gwaetlan gwyaluan vab kilyd (g – l – n/g – l – n/k – l)

Additional examples of Welsh intralinear rime and consonance are presented in Part IV, below.

5

Incidence

All the major ornaments of Old Irish and Old Welsh verse occur in the earliest verse and the earliest linguistic states. No major ornament is confined to a particular verse style or verse form. Alliteration occurs freely in all forms; rime, consonance and assonance occur frequently in the *shamanistic* verse, and at least occasionally even in the Irish *alliterative accentual*. The same system of ornament (based on phonetics and stress) appears in the oldest surviving forms of both secular and Christian verse.

The *monorime strophe* of indeterminate length is the basic form of early Welsh epic verse, as throughout *Y Gododdin*. That this strophe may greatly antedate its earliest documentation is suggested by the comparative analysis (see Part IV, below) of the Old Welsh and Old French epic strophes.

The stanza in early Welsh verse tends to be triadic, and to employ end monorime, but in combination with internal rime of varied incidence, as may be observed in the examples already quoted (pp. 29-30). Triadic quatrains also occur; and these, as well as triads and couplets, occur within the strophes (already quoted —pp. 23-24) of *Y Gododdin*.

The Indo-European long verse line, which is tripartite, becomes the basis of triadic stanzas within the Old Welsh epic strophe. The use of end rime to mark the structural divisions of the long line (as on pp. 33-34, above) produces triadic stanzas; and these lead easily—through a particular use of internal rime in the third phrase of the long line—to the triadic quatrain.

A piece of old poetry from the Irish saga *Táin Bó Cúalgne* combines two salient traits of early Celtic verse—the incremental repetition so pronounced in early Welsh verse, and the *binding* of verse units by aural correspondence between the last word of one verse unit and the first word of the next. Both the incremental repetition and the *binding* are obtained by repetition of an entire word rather than by alliteration or some other ornament:

Móra maitne.
maitne Mide.
móra ossud
ossud Cullend.
móra cundscliu.
cundscliu Chlathra.
móra echrad.
echrad Assail.
móra tedmand.
tedmand tuath Bressi.
móra in chlóe
clóe Ulad im Chonchobar.   TBC,   pp. 707–709

An early Welsh stanza with similar word repetition at the beginning of alternate lines has been previously quoted (p. 36). Such word repetitions could well have characterized a common corpus of Celtic verse that antedated the Celtic occupations of Britain and Ireland. Subsequently to these occupations, Welsh verse continued to refine the technique of incremental repetition; and Irish verse refined the technique of *binding* alliteration. In highly developed forms, these techniques tend to exclude each other. At a rudimentary level, they can obviously merge.

Of two poems attributed to Amorgen, the poet of the Milesian invaders of Ireland, *binding* by word repetition appears throughout one and repetition of grammatical pattern throughout the other, in a manner comparable to the incremental repetition of early Welsh verse.

Amorgen's Incantation, supposedly a spell wrought to ensure the Milesian conquest, is notable as an example of *conachlonn*—the linking of consecutive lines by the use of the last word of one line as the first word of the next:

Ailim iath n-erend
Ermac muir motach
Motach sliab sreatach
Sreatach coill ciotach
Ciotach ab eascach
Easach loc lindmar
Lindmar tor tiopra
Tiopra tuath aenach

Aenach righ teamra
Teamair tor tuatach
Tuata mac milead
Mile long libearn
Libearn ard Ere
Ere ard diclass
Eber dond digbas
Diceadal ro gaet
Ro gaet ban breissi
Breissi ban buaich
[Be nadbail heriu]
Herimon or tus [hir]
hir Eber ailseas
Ailim iath n-erend[5]

It will be observed that alliteration may be used in this poem as a substitute linking device for word repetition; for example, n-*e*rend *e*rmac (lines 1–2), *d*igbas *d*iceadal (lines 15–16), *b*uaich *b*e (lines 18–19). Further, consonance and assonance are also admissible as linking devices. Lines 14 and 15 are not joined in the usual manner, but by a complete parallelism of sound-harmony: the first, second and third words of both lines correspond closely with each other in assonance and consonance, with *diclass* and *digbas* actually riming. Notice also that the last line repeats the first. It was customary for the last word or line of an Irish poem to repeat or else echo the first.

Amorgen's Hymn is distinguished for a continuous entrance-rime that reflects the strict repetition of a grammatical structure:

Amgaeth i*m*muir   amtonn tretha*in*
amfuam i*m*muir   amdam setham
amse*íg fo*raill   amder gréne
amcain lubai   am hé illind.
amloch imaig   ambri dane
amgae lafodb feras fechtu
amde delbas do chínd cotnu
coíche nedgleid clochor slebe
cian cotgair aesa aisci
ciadu illaig fuiniud gréne . . .[6]

The tendency of the last word in the short verses to assonate with the last word of the short verse written below it should be noted, as also the tendency toward alliterative correspondence and end-assonance in the long verse.

The language of the poems attributed to Amorgen is corrupt in the manuscripts, though recognizably Old Irish. The original language of the poems may not have been Old Irish, however, but the proto-Goidelic of the ogham inscriptions. Because of the substance of the poems it is tempting to find that their antiquity is responsible for their corrupt manuscript tradition and their imperfection—at one or two places, according to possibly later rules—in some of the graces of rime and assonance. Although two short poems could hardly be expected to furnish a full exemplification of early indigenous devices, the poems attributed to Amorgen in fact illustrate two salient principles of Old Irish verse ornament: *Amorgen's Incantation*, the linking of consecutive lines through a correspondence between the end of one and the beginning of the other; and *Amorgen's Hymn*, the linking of consecutive verse units through a parallelism of sound-harmony.

Ornament such as rime, consonance and assonance serves as an alternate to alliteration (or to word repetition) for linkage or correspondence in the poems quoted above, and in others of comparable style. For example, another short poem from the *Táin* shows clearly that end-rime or end-assonance compensated as a linking device for alliteration between the last word of one line and the first word of the next:

> Crenaid brain
> braigde fer
> bruinden fuil
> feochair cath
> coinmuid luind
> mesctuich tuind
> taib imthuill
> im nithgalaib
> iar luimnich
> luud fianna
> fetal ferda
> fir Cruachan
> cotas-crith
> immardbith.   TBC,   p. 831

The fifth and sixth lines are linked by perfect end-rime, *luind*, *tuind*, in lieu of an alliterative link between the end word of the fifth and the first word of the sixth. The last two lines are linked by rime (cr*ith*, b*ith*) and assonance (on *a*) and for the same reason. The echoes within the lines of this poem and between consecutive lines are especially rich: either rime, assonance, or consonance ties almost every word to its neighbours. For example, in lines 1–3, cren*aid* rimes with *brain*, and *brain* with *braigde*. *Braigde* assonates with f*er*, and f*er* rimes with bruind*en*. *Braigde fer* consonates with *bruinden fuil*, and br*uinde*n rimes with f*uil*. Then, in lines 7–8 and 8–9, the four words of each pair assonate and partly rime inversely, the first and fourth words corresponding with each other (t*aib*, nithgal*aib*, *iar fianna*); and the second and third words, also with each other (*im*thuill *im*, *luimn*ich *luud*). Inverse correspondences of this character are employed in *Amra Choluimb Chille*.

The learned poets (*filid*) originally exercised the functions of prophet, diviner and enchanter. By Caesar's time, these functions had apparently become specialized, inasmuch as Caesar refers to separate classes of druid, and there are Irish terms for these classes, analogous to Caesar's terms. An equal specialization may be safely assumed for the Celtic islands: Caesar indicates that druidism was most highly developed there, and recent scholarship tends to find that druidism originated in the Celtic isles, though the issue must be held open, if only in view of Strabo's references to the Galatae.

Druidic curses and satires are instructive as to both druidism and verse ornament. A few examples will establish the role of shamanistic parallelism in relation to the Old Irish use of rime, consonance and assonance. The following prophecy, purportedly druidic, concerning the coming of Patrick illustrates how the repetition of grammatical structure can contribute to richness in parallel interlacement of assonance and rime between two or more verse lines:

ticfa tal-cend	Adze-head will come
dar muir merr-cend,	over mad-head sea,
a brat toll-cend,	his cloak hole-head,
a chrand crom-cend,	his staff crook-head,
a mias i n-iarthair (a thige) huile	his table in the west of his house;
frigserat [fris·gerat] a muinter	All his household will answer
huile am*en* am*en* lh I, p. 100[7]	Amen, Amen. lh II, p. 81

There is continuous assonance on *a* at the opening of lines; and on *e*, at their close. All six lines contain alliteration, assonance or rime. The first four lines end on the same syllable; and the last two lines, on the same word.

The 'first satire made in Ireland' is a shamanistic curse or spell:

> Cen cholt for crib cernini,
> cen gert ferbba fora n-asa aithrinni,
> cen adba fir iar ndruba disoirchi,
> cen díl daimi rissi,
> ro sain Brisse. BACC, p. 158[8]

> Without food speedily on a platter,
> without a cow's milk whereon a calf thrives,
> without a man's habitation after the staying of darkness,
> without payment of a band of story-tellers,
> be that (the fate) of Bres! BACC, p. 159

As with the druidic prophecy, a grammatical parallelism is reflected in a parallelism of alliteration, assonance and rime. The lines of the satire being longer, the poet has more scope for a variety of device. Hence, in addition to almost continuous entrance rime and dissyllabic end-rime, the verse displays a link of alliteration between the last word of each line and the first word, following the entrance rime, of the next; for example, cernini *g*ert, *a*ithrinni *a*dba, *d*isoirchi *d*íl; except that, since there is no entrance rime joining the last two lines, the link in the last line is supplied by the first word of the line. Further, each line except the last, which contains a proper name, has at least one pair of alliterating words.

The insistent rhythmic repetition of grammatical patterns in the shamanistic verse, when attended by repetition or correspondence of sounds, must have worked powerfully on the primitive psyche to effect the emotional states and the trances attributable to the shaman's words of power. In this verse, parallelism of ornament is sometimes utilized together with alliterative links between the end of one line or half-line and the beginning of the next. The various kinds of rime and its variants, and the various modes of alliteration, are thus drawn upon mutually to intensify the poet-magician's web of harmonious or hypnotic sound.

C

A 'poem written to raise blisters' also exhibits the characteristic pagan Irish prosodic devices of an alliterative link between the end and beginning of consecutive lines, and of continuous rime at the beginning and end of grammatical units and verse units. The poem is preserved, in somewhat different versions, in manuscripts of *Cormac's Glossary*. Its original setting was an old Irish saga.

> Maile baire gaire Caieur
> combeodutar celtra cath Caier
> Caier dibá Caier dira Caier foró
> fomara fochara Caier.[9]

> Evil, death, and short life to Caier;
> May spears of battle slay Caier;
> The rejected of the land and earth is Caier;
> Beneath the mounds and the rocks be Caier.[10]

Notice the use of the name *Caier* to provide the end-rime in lines one, two and four; the entrance rime among the three phrases of line three; the link between the end of line two and the beginning of line three. Other graces are: (1) link alliteration on *c* between the end of line one and the beginning of line two; (2) the same sort of link on *f* between lines three and four; (3) the inlaid rime in line one—*maile baire gaire Cai*eur; (4) the inlaid rimes in lines three and four—*dibá/dira, fomara/fochara*; (5) the alliteration internal to each line. There is not a single word in the four lines that is not linked in one or more ways to corresponding or adjoining words in the same or adjoining lines.

Is it permissible to regard prayer—pagan prayer—as essentially shamanistic? Especially if, by formulas of invocation, such prayer attempts to bind the higher powers? A splendid specimen has survived, with the help of a Christian tag—a pagan prayer for long life:

> Admuiniur secht n-ingena [trethan]
> dolbte snáthi macc n-āesmar.
> Trī bās ūaim rohuccaiter!
> tri āes dom dorataiter!
> secht tonna tacid dom doradailter!

Nīmchollet messe fom chūairt
i llūrig lasrēin cen lēniud!
Ni nascthar mo chlū ar chel!
domthī āes, nīmthī bās corba sen.

Admuiniur m'argetnia nad ba nad bebe:
amser dom doridnastar findruni febe.
 Rohorthar mo richt,
 rosōerthar mo recht,
 romōrthar mo lecht,
 nīmthī bās for fecht,
 rofīrthar mo thecht!
Nīmragba nathir dīchonn
nā dorb dūrglass
nā dōel dīchuinn!
Nīmmillethar teol
nā cuire ban nā cuire buiden!
domthī aurchur n-amsire ō Rīg inna n-uile!

Admuiniur Senach sechtamserach
conaltar mnā sīde for bruinnib būais.
 Nī bāiter mo ṡechtchaindel!
 Am dūn dīthogail,
 am ail anscuichthe,
 am lia lōgmar,
 am sēn sechtmainech.
 Ropo chētach cētblīadnach,
 cech cēt diib ar ūair!
Cotagaur cucum mo lessa:
robē rath in spiurto nōib form-sa!
Domini est salus, ter, Christi est salus, ter.
Super populum tuum, Domine, benedictio tua.

I invoke the seven daughters of the Sea,
who fashion the threads of the sons of long life.
 May three deaths be taken from me!
 May three periods of age be granted to me!
 May seven waves of good fortune be dealt to me!
Phantoms shall not harm me on my journey
in flashing corslet without hindrance.
My fame shall not perish.
May old age come to me! death shall not come to me till I am old.

I invoke my Silver Champion who has not died, who will not die.
May a time be granted to me of the quality of white bronze!
   May my double be slain!
   May my right be maintained!
   May my strength be increased!
   Let my grave not be ready!
Death shall not come to me on an expedition.
May my journey be carried to an end!
The headless adder shall not seize me,
nor the hard-grey worm,
nor the headless black chafer.
Neither thief shall harm me,
nor band of women, nor a band of armed men.
Let increase of time come to me from the King of the Universe!

I invoke Senach of the seven periods of time,
whom fairy women have reared on the breasts of plenty.
   May my seven candles be not extinguished!
   I am an indestructible stronghold,
   I am an unshaken rock,
   I am a precious stone,
   I am the luck of the week.
May I live a hundred times a hundred years,
each hundred of them apart!
I summon their boons to me.
May the grace of the *holy spirit* be upon me!
Domini est salus (*three times*), Christi est salus (*three times*)
Super populum tuum, Domine, benedictio tua [Ps. 3 v. 9]

MMH, pp. 19—21.

In this prayer, the compositional technique is basically parallelism rather than linkage of contiguous terminals. Though alliteration occurs as an ornament within almost every line, the verse structure of the prayer is underlined chiefly by rime and assonance at the opening or close, or both, of consecutive lines.

In some respects, the elegies attributed to Dallan Forgaill, *Amra Senain* and *Amra Choluimb Chille*, constitute a summation of the techincal features of Old Irish verse. *Amra Choluimb Chille* combines traits of the versification and ornament of the *alliterative accentual*, *shamanistic* and *riming stanzaic* styles.

The following quotation from *Amra Senain* illustrates the main features of its alliterative technique, and the basic principles of the more involved technique of *Amra Choluimb Chille*:

5. Ruide im rochorp carcrastar cen chais modeat
   mugsaine is macc Geirrgind gart.

6. Glainidir gol go noam som súi dian sossad
   sidlotha sine i Cathaig caur.

7. Cáin n-ard n-orddon n-adamra assa ordon
   archaingel hi findmaigeib fil.

8. Fiadh fochraice follnathar amru cach ór oeibligad
   ina ma[ni mo].

9. Mor ua Dubtaig drongo(blaig) dom ro[ḟ]oir
   dom rusc reil-cobair ar a molta míad.

10. Moai mo rosc rigfotha mo da n hed
    n-ard n-imchaissen uassnaib nim-combeb[a]blái.

11. Bleasc amrosc ilarda co mbrosnaigib uath
    uas mo luirgnib langlassaib is forru mada fail.[11]

It is evident that the prosodic ideal—not invariably achieved—is a linkage of each word with its neighbours, chiefly by means of alliteration, but also by means of assonance, consonance and rime. Alliteration is practically compulsory between the last word of one long line and the first word of the next. Thus, *gart-glainidir* (lines 5–6), *caur-cain* (lines 6–7), *fil-fiadh* (lines 7–8), etc. Alliteration is also extremely common within the verse line, within the sense units of this line, and between the last word of one sense unit and the first word of the next.

Amra Choluimb Chille displays less rigidity and more variety of technique than *Amra Senain*, more virtuosity in its parallelism, and some linking devices not exploited in *Amra Senain*. The opening lines of *Amra Choluimb Chille*, following the prefatory stanza, provide some suggestions of the technical differences between the two poems:

Ni disceoil dúe Neill.
Ni huctot oenmaige. / Mor ma[i]rg. / Mor deilm

Diḟulaing riss re aisneid, Colum cen beith, cen chill
Co india dui dó? sceo Nera BACC, pp. 156–160

Notice first the linking of successive lines and phrases by an
elementary sort of entrance-rime, a repetition of the identical
word at the opening, reflecting a rhetorical parallelism: *ni-ni,
mor-mor*. The presence of this entrance-rime obviates the requirement of a link between the last word of one line or phrase and the
first word of the next. Proper names are not subject to the rules;
hence *Colum*, above, does not respond to any word immediately
preceding it. Notice also the correspondence between the first
and last words of some phrases—'*Ni* disceoil dúe *Neill*', '*Co* india
dui d*ó*'. Indeed, there is an inverse echo in these phrases—*n, d,
d, n; o, d, d, o*. Then, observe the expansion of the sound of Colum
Cille's name in another phrase—*Colum* cen beith, cen *chill*.

A freer use of assonance and rime distinguishes *Amra Choluimb
Chille* from *Amra Senain*. Not only does assonance substitute
frequently as a linking device, instead of alliteration, between
the end word of one line and the first word of the next, but it
also appears as a link between the end words of successive phrases.
And rime itself is also used in this manner. Here is an example
of assonance replacing the conventional alliterative link between
lines:

> Atruic roard trath Dé do Cholum cui*techta*
> Finn*fethal* fre*stal*   BACC,   p. 166

The following is an example of assonance between the end words of
consecutive phrases:

> di*f*ulaing riss re aisn*ei*d
> Colum cen b*ei*th   BACC,   pp. 158–160

The following is an example of end-rime linking corresponding lines
and phrases:

> Grés ro fer fechtn*achu*
> Fri *arthu* arch*athru*
> co domun *dringthiar*
> Ar deo doen*achta*
> Ar assaib *rigthi*[a]r   BACC,   pp. 260–262[12]

The first and fourth lines are linked by end-rime, as are the third
and fifth; and the second line contains an internal chime. Assonance
links the second with the first and fourth lines.

Another technical feature of *Amra Choluimb Chille* is its use of two linking devices in the same passage. In the following extract, entrance-rime joins a series of phrases that are also connected by alliteration and rime between the last word of one phrase and the second word of the succeeding phrase:

> *Boe* saegul *sneid*
> *Boe seim sáth*
> *Boe sab* suithe ce*ch dind*
> *Boe dind* oc libur leigdocht   BACC,   p. 168

Alliteration is also used as a link between the opening of phrases, and, as such, it may be combined with a second linking device:

> La*ss*ais tír *tuaith*
> Lei*ss tuath* occidens   BACC,   pp. 168–170

Alliterative inversion such as appears within the opening line of the body of the poem is also used as a device linking consecutive lines:

> *C*otrolass *O*riens
> *O ch*leirchib *c*ridochtaib   BACC,   p. 170

Assonance appears as an entrance link:

> *C*otrolass *O*riens
> *O* chleirchib cridochtaib
> F*ó* dibath   BACC,   p. 170

Both the opening and close of consecutive lines may be linked, and the end link may exist between a final in one line and a penultimate word in the next:

> *Ranic* iath nad adaig aiccesd*ar.*
> *Ranic* tir do Moise muinemm*ar.*   BACC,   p. 172
> *Ranic* maige mos nad genat*ar* ciuil   BACC,   p. 174

The tendency to link as richly as possible may result in a parallelism so complete as to include every sound of two consecutive phrases:

> Ba dín do nochtaib
> Ba did do bochtaib   BACC,   p. 268

As in *Amra Senain*, the presence of alliteration throughout a phrase or line usually involves the use of a different device for linking these units:

> R*ai*th rith rethes
> Dar *cais cai*ndenam
> F*aig* feirb fithir   BACC,   p. 248
> G*ais* gluassa gle   BACC,   p. 252

Finally, as in *Amra Senain*, all the devices that link verse serve to link not only sense units, but words within these units. Alliteration throughout the phrase: the first, third and fourth lines just quoted. Inverse alliteration within the phrase has already been indicated in the opening line of the body of the poem. It occurs elsewhere also; for example, *ba did do bochtaib*, above. Assonance occurs throughout the phrase—mi*ad* m*ar* munim*ar* m*anna* (mi*ad mar*—imperfect assonance; see p. 47). Consonance sometimes appears within the phrase—*ni foet na fua*cht, *ni* oe*ned ni na bu, beo a ainm beo a anuaim*; alliteration, rime and assonance—Ro*anic a*xalu la *airbriu ar*ch*angliu*.

The two introductory quatrains of Dallan Forgaill's *Amra Choluimb Chille* are composed in a quasi-syllabic measure. These quatrains embody the same system of verse ornament as *Brigit be bithmaith* (discussed below). It is therefore doubly significant that good critical opinion accepts *Amra Choluimb Chille* for what it purports to be—a composition written shortly after the death of Colum Cille in 597 AD.[13] Here are the two introductory quatrains:

> Dīa Dīa dorrogus re tīas inna gnūis   culu tre nēit.
> Dīa nime nīmreilge i llurgu i n-ēgthiar   ar mūichthea mēit.
> Dīa mār m'anacul de muir theintidiu   diudercc ndēr.
> Dīa fīriēn fīrocus cluinethar mo donuāil   de nemīath nēl.
> MMH,   p. 27

The end-rime joining the pair of short lines in each quatrain is perfect. Less noticeable, possibly, are the links of alliteration binding the last word of each long line with the first word of its following short line (*g*nuis:*c*ulu, *e*gthiar:*a*r, *th*eintidiu:*d*iudercc, *d*onuail:*d*e). These links are also assonantal in the first three pairs.

Alliteration graces each long line, and entrance-rime on *Dia* links the long lines. Each couplet is linked to the next by alliteration between the last word of the couplet and the second word or first word of the next couplet: *n*eit *n*ime, *m*eit *m*ar, *n*der *D*ia. The linking with the second word rather than the first, as with the first and second, and the second and third couplets, is a device usually employed when the opening word of a line (or couplet) makes entrance-rime with the opening word of the preceding line (or couplet). Dallan Forgaill employs this device later in his poem also, where the opening words of certain successive lines make entrance-rime.

From the evidence of Old Irish legal and prosodic tracts, stanzaic forms—and especially quatrains of the kinds associated immemorially with folk lyric—appear to have been preeminently the concern of the bards, the poets of the folk as distinguished from the learned poets or *filid*. Under the inspiration of democratizing Christianity, the druidic schools declined and the prestige of bardism rose. This circumstance led the *filid* to an increased interest in bardic measures, for economic as well as aesthetic reasons; just as, a millennium later, when traditional Irish society was disintegrating under pressure of imperialism, the learned poets abandoned their recondite and ornate (yet once bardic) syllabic measures, for the accentual assonance of a folk verse that had subsisted for centuries at social levels beneath the notice of druidic inheritors.

By their structure, stanzaic forms suggest or impose distinctive styles of ornament. Rime, for example, tends to become compulsory at set placements; and alliteration tends to become optional. Yet this tendency is not absolute in Old Irish verse. Poems survive in rimeless stanzas whose lines are uniform in syllable count. Richly riming poems also survive whose quatrains are not measurable syllab-ically. Poems survive whose rime scheme varies from stanza to stanza.

Though Old Irish genealogical verse chiefly employs *alliterative accentual* paragraphs of indeterminate length, it also employs stanzaic form: some genealogical poems have rimeless quatrains with lines of uniform syllable count; while others have richly riming irregular quatrains. The genealogical poems continue an indigenous style. The christianization of Ireland does not appear to have affected their technique, although it led to the extension backward of certain genealogies for the inclusion of such biblical worthies as Adam.

The following genealogical poem combines the principal features of *alliterative-accentual* and *riming-stanzaic* verse:

1 Nida dīr dermait   dāla cach rīg rōmdai,
   reimse rīg Temro   tūatha for slicht slōgdai.

2 Sōer cathmīl cōemḟata   Mōen Labraid Loṅgsech,
   leo nīthach, nathchobir,   cathchobir comsech.

3 Cāinmīl Ailill fri āga   fri crīcha Crothomuin,
   crothais Abratchāin   airbe īath nEthomuin.

MAID, I, pp. 16–17

The combination of compulsory dissyllabic end-rime with compulsory end-link alliteration is notable for its virtuosity, especially considering the richness also of intralinear consonance, assonance and alliteration.

The most adroit poem, technically, in the entire range of Old Irish Christian verse was written in praise of St Brigid. This Old Irish poem, which apparently antedates comparably styled Hiberno-Latin verse, embodies a greater variety and richness of ornament, within a riming stanza of more compressed compass, than anything subsequently written in Hiberno-Latin. Not only is there remarkable virtuosity of ornament internal to stanzas: all six stanzas relate to each other in paired correspondences, resulting in an intricacy of interrelation that compares to the complex interweaving of design in such masterpieces of manuscript illumination as the *Book of Kells*. A close analysis of the ornament in *Brigit be bithmaith* is justified not only by its artistic profusion but also because its adroitness provides a standard by which to measure the gradual approach to it of the Hiberno-Latin hymns in praise of saints.

The following array indicates links between successive lines. Alliteration provides approximately one-half of these links; assonance and consonance, in equal measure, provide almost all the rest. The links occur typically, though not exclusively, between the end word of one line and the first word of the next.

Brigit bé *b*ithmaith
*b*reō *órde* óiblech,
*d*on*fé* don *b*ithflaith
in grén tind *tóidl*ech.

Ronsóira Brigit   (*ronsoira, roroina*)
se*ch* *drungu* demne:
ro*ró*ina re*u*nn   (*ronsoira, roroina*)
cath*u* cach *th*edme.

*D*irodba *in*diunn
ar colno *c*ísu
in *ch*róib co *mbláthib*
in *máthir* Ísu.

*I*nd fíróg *inmain*
co *n*ordd*on* ad*b*il,
*b*é sóir cech *inbaid*
la*m nóib* di *L*aignib.

*L*ethcholbe f*l*atho
la Patricc pr*ím*de
in tlacht ós *lígib*
ind *rígin rígde*.

*R*obet *ér* sin*it*
ar *cuirp* hi *c*ilicc;
d*ia* rath *ron*bróina
*ron*sóira Brigit   STP,   pp. 325–326[14]

The following array indicates the intralinear consonance (italicized)
and the intralinear alliteration (bold):

Brigit **b**é **b**i*th*maith   (*bith*/*maith*)
*b*reō **ó**rde **ó**i*b*lech,
donfé **d**on *b*ith*fl*aith (*bith*/*flaith*)
in grén **t**ind **t**ói*dl*ech.

Ronsóira **Br**igit
sech **d**rung*u* **d**em*n*e:
ror*ó*ina **r**eu*nn*
cath*u* **c**ach thedme.

Diro*db*a i*n*diu*nn*
ar **c**ol*n*o **c**ísu
in **ch**ró*ib* **c**o *mb*láth*ib* (*nchr*, *mbl*)
i*n* máth*ir* **Í**su.

Ind **f**í**r**óg **i**n*main* (*nd, rg, nm, n*)
co n**o**r*ddon* **a**d*bil,*
b**é** s**ó***ir* c*ech* in**b**a*id* (*oir, in ; ech, aid*)
l*am* n**ó**i*b* di **L**a*ignib.*

Let*h*cholbe f*latho*
la **P**a*tricc* p*rímd*e
in *t*lach*t* ós l*íg*ib
ind **r**í*gin* **r**í*gd*e.   (*ind, in ; rig, rigd*)

R**o**be*t ér* s*init*
ar **c**u*irp* hi **c**i*licc*;
dia **r**ath **r**on**b**r**ó**in*a* (*ron/broin*a)
ron*sói*ra **B**rigit

Though its author limits himself to a line of only five syllables
there are normally at least two ornaments—one being alliteration—
in each line.   Then, each line is linked to its following line by
devices characteristically placed, the link being particularly pronounced between the last word of each quatrain and the first word
of the next.   The last word of the poem is also its first, in conformity
with the Irish rules for finishing a poem, and the last two words
are the first two of the second quatrain.   In all six quatrains, the
second and fourth lines are joined by end-rime that is dissyllabic,
accentual and (normally) perfect.   Further, the quatrains themselves
are patterned according to the character of the end-rime that
appears in them: the first and fourth quatrains display dissyllabic
end-rime (imperfect in the fourth quatrain) between the first
and third lines as well as the second and fourth; and in both
quatrains the final consonants correspond in the first and second,
and the third and fourth, lines; the second and fifth quatrains
display, in the last word of their third line, a link of assonance
between the accented vowel of this word and the accented vowel of
the riming end words of the second and fourth lines; the third and
sixth quatrains display a similar correspondence between the end
word of the first line and the riming end words of the second and
fourth lines, the correspondence in the sixth quatrain actually
constituting rime.   Notice that in all three pairs of corresponding
quatrains the correspondences are of a different character as among
the pairs and that, even within each pair, the correspondence

consists in similarity and not identity of device. Thus in the first
quatrain the end-rime is perfect, but in the fourth it is imperfect;
in the second quatrain the end-link in the third line is purely one of
assonance, but in the fifth quatrain the link also involves the consonants surrounding the assonating vowel (*prímd*e, *lig*ib, *rigd*e);
in the third quatrain the link, although dissyllabic, is again assonance
(*indiu*nn, *cisu*), but in the sixth quatrain it is rime (si*nit*, *cilic*).

The stylistic intention of *Brigit be bithmaith* cannot be mistaken.
By the use of traditional devices its author sought the utmost
in balanced intensity of sound-harmony, and this within the limits
of a five-syllable verse line. The artistic ideal was the creation
of a web of sound in which each line, each word, each syllable,
each consonant and each vowel bear an aural and structural relationship to their neighbours or to corresponding elements of the
same rank.

The scholiastic preface to the poem in the *Liber Hymnorum* lists
five possible authors—four from the sixth century, and one who
died no later than 656 AD. Linguistically, there appears to be
no objection to a sixth-century origin.

St Colmán mac Léníni, Abbot of Cloyne, who died in 604, was
first a professional poet. His praise poem for a sword given
him by Domnall (later king of Tara), composed early—before
Colmán's conversion, further testifies to pagan Irish use of the
same rhythm, form and ornament as appears in the praise poem for
Brigid:

1. Luin oc elaib
   Ungi oc dírnaib
   Drecha ban n-aithech
   Oc ródaib rignaib

2. Ríg oc Domnall
   Dord oc aidbse
   Adand oc caindil
   Calg oc mo chailg-se

OSHI, p. 24

6

Hiberno-Latin Verse Ornament

The chronology of the styles of Hiberno-Latin poetry can be established with a satisfactory degree of probability. The early styles of this poetry, save for the riming quantitative, are all represented in two Irish sources, The *Antiphonary of Bangor*, which dates from the late seventh century, and the *Liber Hymnorum*, which is preserved in manuscripts of the eleventh century. The major portion of the *Liber Hymnorum* represents transcriptions of documents one or two centuries older; and perhaps these sources were themselves, chiefly, transcriptions.

Most of the hymns in the *Liber Hymnorum*, both Latin and Irish, are accompanied with scholiastic prefaces, which usually furnish information as to the composition of the hymns. These prefaces, though not really critical, present traditions, sometimes frankly conflicting, regarding the authors of the hymns. Some of these traditions, at first hastily dismissed as unfounded, have been taken more seriously as a result of closer study. For example, the scholiastic declaration that St Sechnall was the son of a Lombard of Letha was once doubted on the ground that there were no Lombards in Brittany during the fifth century. Nevertheless, we do know of their presence there at that time.[15] Consequently, when in the *Liber Hymnorum* a scholiast lists five possible authors for a hymn—none of whom died later than 656 AD—there is good basis for inferring the existence of a common tradition of sixth- or seventh-century authorship, and some basis for crediting the tradition.

Critical opinion until recently had accepted the *Hymn in Praise of St Patrick* attributed to St Sechnall, reputedly a nephew of Patrick, as probably the oldest available Hiberno-Latin poem. Recently the poem has been shown to be a mid-sixth-century forgery, made in the interest of Armagh's claims to ecclesiastical primacy. Its opening verses follow:

Audite omnes amantes
Deum sancta merita
Viri in Christo beati,
Patricii episcopi,
Quomodo bonum ob actum
Similatur angelis,
Perfectamque propter vitam
Æquatur apostolis.

Beata in Christi custodit
Mandata in omnibus,
Cujus opera refulgent
Clara inter homines,
Sanctumque cujus sequuntur
Exemplum mirificum,
Unde et in cœlis Patrem
Magnificant Dominum.   AB II,   p. 14[16]

Considerable end-consonance and end-assonance are present, though no regular patterning is sustained. In the last twelve lines quoted, it may appear that alternate lines tend to consonate roughly. If this was the poet's conscious intention, he did not sustain it in succeeding stanzas. Nevertheless, the first seven stanzas—as a typical sample—disclose, within the quatrain, identical end-letters in thirty-two of the fifty-six lines, identical end-vowels in thirty-one of the fifty-six, and identical final accented vowels in twenty-two of the fifty-six. Alliteration is fairly frequent in terms of the Irish rules which, of course, may not apply.

A communion hymn associated with St Sechnall exhibits the same style of verse ornament as characterizes *Audite omnes amantes*:

Sancti venite,
Christi corpus sumite,
Sanctum bibentes
Quo redempte sanguinem.

Salvati Christi
Corpore et sanguine,
A quo refecti
Laudes dicamus Deo.

AB II,   p. 10;   RCLP,   pp   0–71

The eleven stanzas disclose, within the quatrain unit, identical end-letters in twenty-three of the forty-four lines, identical end-vowels also in twenty-three of the forty-four, and identical final accented vowels in nine of the forty-four. Alliteration is fairly frequent.

In the character and the proportional frequency of riming devices, the two hymns associated with St Sechnall resemble the hymns of St Ambrose. In these there is the same marked tendency toward identity in the end-vowels, end-letters and end-syllables of the lines within each of the four-line stanzas, and toward a lesser but still evident degree of correspondence in the final accented vowels of the lines. *Deus creator omnium,* by Ambrose, reflects these tendencies:

Deus creator omnium
polique rector, vestiens
diem decoro lumine,
noctem soporis gratia;

artus solutos ut quies
reddat laboris usui,
mentesque fessas allevet
luctusque solvat anxios;

grates peracto jam die
et noctis exortu preces,
voti reos ut adjuves,
hymnum canentes solvimus.

te cordis ima concinant,
te vox canora concrepet,
te diligat castus amor,
te mens adoret sobria;

ut, cum profunda clauserit
diem caligo noctium,
fides tenebras nesciat
et nox fide reluceat.

dormire mentem ne sinas,
dormire culpa noverit;
castis fides refrigerans
somni vaporem temperet.

exuta sensu lubrico
te cordis ima somnient,
nec hostis invidi dolo
pavor quietos suscitet.

Christum rogemus et Patrem,
Christi Patrisque Spiritum,
unum potens per omnia,
fove precantes, Trinitas.   RCLP,   pp. 11–12

Of the thirty-two lines, twenty lines are identical—within the four-line stanza—in end-letters; nineteen are identical in end-vowels; six are identical in end-syllables; and twelve are identical in final accented vowels.   In the other three hymns unquestionably written by Ambrose, the proportion of identity is slightly lower as regards end-letters and end-vowels, and slightly higher as regards end-syllables and final accented vowels.   But these identities or correspondences do not appear in a regular fashion within the stanza, nor is there pattern among the stanzas as a whole respecting these correspondences.   Ambrose finds his 'rimes' as well as he can, and with somewhat more regard for final letters and vowels than for final accented vowels.   In short, the correspondences are not regularly patterned.

The hymns unquestionably by Ambrose and the hymns attributed to Sechnall are so similar in the proportion of identical letters, end-vowels, end-syllables and final accented vowels within the quatrain unit, that they may be regarded as specimens of a single style of verse ornament.   This style approaches but does not achieve a systematic use of either rime or assonance.

In at least one poem of Sedulius (fifth century), this style approaches very closely to systematic rime.   Though *A solis ortus cardine* presents no sustained rime scheme, it offers an irregular succession of rough approximations to several stanzaic rime schemes that were employed throughout whole lyrics in later times, both in Latin and in the various vernaculars:

A solis ortus cardine
adusque terrae limitem
Christum canamus principem,
natum Maria virgine.

Beatus auctor saeculi
servile corpus induit,
ut carne carnem liberans
non perderet quod condidit.

Clausae parentis viscera
caelestis intrat gratia
venter puellae baiulat
secreta quae non nouerat.

Domus pudici pectoris
templum repente fit dei,
intacta nesciens virum
verbo creavit filium.

Enixa est puerpera
quem Gabrihel praedixerat,
quem matris alvo gestiens
clausus Iohannes senserat.

Faeno iacere pertulit,
praesepe non abhorruit,
parvoque lacte pastus est,
per quem nec ales esurit.

Gaudet chorus caelestium,
et angeli canunt deum,
palamque fit pastoribus
pastor creatorque omnium. RCLP, pp. 39–42

Stanzas structurally identical with those of Ambrose are employed;
yet the poem is far richer than any of the unquestionably authentic
poems of Ambrose in identity of end-letters, end-vowels, end-
syllables and even final accented vowels. A number of the identities
involve the final two and sometimes three vowels, and occasionally
even the consonants syllabically bound with these vowels.

The *Antiphonary of Bangor* includes a number of hymns that follow the style of verse ornament characteristic of Ambrose and Sechnall. From the structure of the *Antiphonary*, these hymns were evidently employed in the monastic offices. Hence it is likely that the hymns are considerably older than the date of the *Antiphonary*.

Two of these hymns are 'Ambrosian' in stanzaic structure. *Hymnus Mediae Noctis* (AB II, 46–48) is familiar from other sources, and may well be a work of Ambrose. *Hymnus quando Cereus Benedicitur* (AB II, 11) is known from no other source; but this circumstance is not enough to establish Irish authorship. Though considerable alliteration occurs within the verse line of this hymn the alliteration does not have, consistently, an Irish character. In both these hymns the 'rime' is of the mixed variety already remarked in Ambrose and Sechnall. There is no patterning of end-correspondences, and the types of correspondence are of the same character and of substantially the same proportional frequency as in the hymns by Ambrose.

Another of the Bangor hymns, *Hymnus Sancti Camelaci*, is structurally identical with *Audite omnes amantes*. *Camelacus* was one of the bishops consecrated by St Patrick, but there is no way of determining the precise date of the hymn. Its first two stanzas follow:

> Audite bonum exemplum
> Benedicti pauperis
> Camelaci Cumiensis
> Dei justi famuli
>
> Exemplum praebet in toto
> Fidelis in opere,
> Gratias deo agens,
> Hilaris in omnibus. AB II, p. 19

Within the quatrain, sixteen of the total twenty-four lines are identical in their final accented vowel; fourteen are identical in their final vowel; and twelve are identical in their final letter. Alliteration seems not to be sought. The rime and assonance in this hymn, though still sporadic, are nearer in richness to Sedulius than to Ambrose.

Hymnus Apostolorum ut alii dicunt, also from the *Antiphonary of Bangor*, is rich in end-correspondence of the mixed variety discovered in the hymns so far analysed; and, as in these, no regular patterning of correspondences is sustained. There is some trace of system, however, and the very moderate amount of alliteration appears to be unsought.

> 1. Precamur patrem
>   Regem omnipotentem,
>   Et Jesum Christum,
>   Sanctum quoque spiritum.
>
> Alleluia

> 3. Universorum
>   Fontis jubar luminum
>   Æthereorum
>   Et orbi lucentium.

> 16. In fine mundi
>   Post tanta mysteria
>   Adest Salvator
>   Cum grandi clementia.   AB II,   pp. 5–6

At least three lines—and usually all four—of almost every quatrain are linked by identity of either end-letter, end-vowel, end-syllable or final accented vowel. Of the 168 lines of the hymn, 112 are identical, within the quatrain, in the end-letter; 121, in the final vowel; 91, in the end-syllable; and 75, in the final accented vowel. Furthermore, correspondence on the final accented vowel occurs with noticeably greater frequency in quatrains that are relatively deficient in one or more of the other types of rime. *Hymnus Apostolorum*, on the whole, is the nearest to systematic rime of all the specimens available from Irish sources of what might be termed 'Ambrosian' verse ornament.

Altus Prosator, ascribed to St Colum Cille, embodies a rime scheme. Good critical opinion confidently attributes the poem to Colum Cille, and thereby assigns it a date no later than the year 597.   (LH II,   pp. 140–146)

A   Altus prosator vetustus
    dierum et ingenitus
    erat absque origine
    primordii et crepidine
    est et erit in saecula
    saeculorum infinita
    cui est unigenitus
    Christus et sanctus spiritus . . .   LH I, p. 66

T   Tuba primi archangeli
    strepente admirabili
    erumpent munitissima
    claustra ac poliandria
    mundi presentis frigora
    hominum liquescentia
    undique conglobantibus
    ad compagines ossibus
    animabus aethralibus
    eisdem obviantibus
    rursumque redeuntibus
    debitis mansionibus   LH I, p. 79

Though the end-rime is regular—often dissyllabic, and sometimes trisyllabic—it is not accentual. Neither is it regular in the number of syllables which it encompasses, nor in the number of successive verse pairs that are joined by an identical end-rime. Further, there is little alliteration and slight trace of the Irish riming of consonants according to class. Classification of vowels for riming purposes is, however, possibly recognized: *us* and *os* are rimed twice; and *i* and *e*, rimed twice in end-syllables, appear several times in the penultimate between syllables that rime. According to the Irish rules, rimes of classed vowels in unstressed syllables are admissible.

A number of early Hiberno-Latin hymns, some attributed to Colum Cille, follow the riming style of *Altus Prosator*. Probably these are not so old as *Altus Prosator*, there being reason to doubt the attribution of various of them to the saint, and the others being best attributed to personages who lived later than he did. It is notable that Irish devices, particularly the characteristic alliteration, appear in most of the available poems that employ

the rime method of the *Altus Prosator*. The following are some lines
from one of these, which may have been composed about the middle
of the seventh century (LH pp. II, 106–107):

> Christus in nostra insola
> quae vocatur hibernia
> ostensus est hominibus
> maximis mirabilibus
> quae perfecit per felicem
> celestis vitae virginem
> praecellentem pro merito
> magno in mundi circulo LH I, p. 14

In the first line, *-ostra* assonates with *-ola*, and both these assonate
with *voca-* in the second line. In the fifth line, *perfecit* consonates
and assonates with *per felic-*. There is alliteration in all lines but
the second, in which a consonance has the effect of alliteration—
quae, -catur. Other graces are no doubt obvious. As in *Altus
Prosator*, the rime is neither accentual, nor syllabically measured
nor based on the Irish classification of consonants.

The *Antiphonary of Bangor* and the *Liber Hymnorum* preserve
poems in Latin that could stand as models of Old-Irish sound-
harmony. One of these, from the *Liber Hymnorum*, is a Hymn
to St Martin, attributed to St Oengus Mac Tipraite, who died—
according to the *Annals of Ulster*—in 745 AD. This hymn rivals
Brigit be bithmaith in profusion of ornament and intricacy of design.
The following quotations of the Hymn to St Martin are intended
to indicate the intralinear ornament and the interlinear links, aside
from the links of end-rime, end-assonance and end-consonance:

Intralinear Ornament	*Devices*
Martine te deprecor	alliteration, assonance
Pro me rogaris patrem	alliteration, consonance
Christum ac spiritum sanctum	alliteration, consonance
Habentem Mariam matrem	alliteration, consonance
Martinus mirus more	alliteration, consonance
Ore laudauit deum	alliteration
Puro corde cantauit	alliteration, consonance
Atque amauit eum	alliteration

Intralinear Ornament	*Devices*
*E*lectus d*ei ui*u*i*	assonance
*Signa sibi sal*u*tis*	alliteration, consonance
	assonance
*D*onauit *deus* pa*cis*	alliteration, consonance,
*M*agnae *atque* uirt*utis*	assonance, consonance
Uerb*um* dei loc*utus*	assonance
Secutus in mand*atis*	consonance, assonance
U*irtutibus impletis*	consonance
Mor*tuis* resuscit*atis*	consonance
*Sanan*s *homin*es lepra	consonance
*C*ura d*u*p*lic*e m*ira*	consonance
*Mag*n*i*tudine *mala*	consonance, alliteration
E*g*retu*dine dira*	consonance
*Deum dom*in*um* nost*rum*	alliteration, consonance
*P*assum *pro* no*bis* m*ire*	alliteration, assonance
U*olun*t*ar*ie pr*opter* n*os*	consonance, assonance
*D*ep*recare* Ma*rtine.*	consonance

LH I,   p. 47

Interlinear Links	*Lines*	*Devices*
*M*artine te de*precor*		
Pro me rogaris patr*em*	1–2	alliteration
*C*hrist*um* ac spiritum		
s*anctum*	2–3	consonance
*H*ab*entem* Mariam *matrem*	3–4	consonance
	4–1	alliteration, consonance
*Martin*us mirus m*ore*		
Ore laud*auit* deum	1–2	rime
Puro *corde* cant*auit*	2–3	rime
Atque am*auit* eum	3–4	rime, assonance
	4–1	alliteration
*E*lectus dei u*iui*		
*S*igna s*ibi* salu*tis*	1–2	rime
*D*ona*uit* deus p*acis*	2–3	assonance, consonance
*M*agnae *atque* u*ir*tutis	3–4	consonance
	4–1	alliteration, consonance

Interlinear Links	*Lines*	*Devices*
*U*er**bum** dei lo**cutus**		
Sec*utus* in man*datis*	1–2	rime
Uir*tut*i**bus** imple*tis*	2–3	alliteration, consonance
Mor*tuis* resuscitatis	3–4	consonance
	4–1	alliteration
*S*anans hom*ines* le*pra*		
C*ura* d*uplice* **m***ira*	1–2	consonance, assonance
Magnitudine mala	2–3	alliteration, assonance
Egretudine *d*ira	3–4	rime, consonance
	4–1	alliteration
*D*eum dominum nostr*um*		
Pass*um* pro nobis m*ire*	1–2	consonance
Uolun*tarie* *propt*er nos	2–3	consonance
De*precare* Martine.	3–4	rime, consonance

The dissyllabic accentual end-rime joining the second and fourth lines of each quatrain is perfect, according to the Irish rules. The final couplet is particularly interesting, since the poet not only closes with the first word of the poem—St Martin's name—but seemingly tries to echo in reverse, as far as possible, the sounds of the opening couplet; that is, the final *e* of *deprecare* echoes *te* in the first line of the poem, and the first three syllables echo *depreco*, and *nos* echoes *pro*, and *propter* reverses *me ro-*, and *-tarie* corresponds with *-garis*, and pa*trem* consonates roughly with *volun-*.

Just as the first and last stanzas are related, so are the second and fifth, and the third and fourth, so that the stanzaic pattern of the poem as a whole is concentric. The relationship between the second and fifth stanzas resides in the similarity of their interlinear linking. In the second stanza, two-word links that are strictly parallel in number of syllables and in rhythm and, to a great degree, in sound unite the second, third and fourth lines (*ore laudavit, corde cantavit, atque amavit*). In the fifth stanza, the parallelism is even more embracing, since it involves all four lines (*homines, duplice, magnitudine, egretudine*). The third and fourth stanzas are related through the fact that their second, third and fourth lines all consonate and assonate on their final syllable (*-tis, -cis*), with the first line in both stanzas tied to the rest by a more tenuous chime on the end-syllable. The inter-stanzaic pattern, however, is more intricate still.

Each stanza of each pair of the related stanzas is itself related through some similarity in the character of its end-harmony to each stanza of another related pair, but so that no single stanza is completely analogous to more than one other. Thus the outermost and innermost pairs are tied through the fact that, in the first and third quatrains, the last three lines end on a common letter. The innermost pair is related to the adjacent pair by the fact that the fourth and fifth stanzas, in all four lines, end on a common letter. The outermost pair is related to the adjacent pair by the fact that the second and sixth quatrains each display end-rime between the second and fourth lines, but close their first and third lines— unlike the other four stanzas—with words unrelated in rime, consonance or assonance either to each other or to the end words of the second and fourth lines.

Inter-stanzaic relationships of the kind that occur in *Brigit be bithmaith* and in the Hymn to St Martin were perhaps intended to achieve effects analogous to those of the illumination in the old Irish manuscripts with their winding bands, divergent spirals and interlaced work.

It will have been observed that in the Hymn to St Martin internal rime and consonance are relied on far more extensively than in *Brigit be bithmaith* to provide interlinear linkage within the quatrain, although both poems rely almost exclusively on alliteration for linkage between quatrains. Other surviving examples of Hiberno-Latin verse exhibit an even more pronounced tendency to rely on devices other than alliteration for interlinear links, not only within the quatrain but between quatrains. At the same time, such poems tend toward a greater reliance on assonance, and on internal rime.

The *Antiphonary of Bangor* preserves a Latin poem that reflects these tendencies, besides embodying some features not present in the poems analysed above; *Versiculi Familiae Benchuir*, indeed, may well be the type or parent of the college song:

> 1. Benchuir bona regula,
>   Recta, atque divina,
>   Stricta, sancta, sedula,
>   Summa, justa, ac mira.

2. Munther Benchuir beata,
   Fide fundata certa,
   Spe salutis ornata,
   Caritate perfecta.

3. Navis numquam turbata,
   Quamvis fluctibus tonsa,
   Nuptiis quoque parata
   Regi domino sponsa.

4. Domus deliciis plena,
   Super petram constructa,
   Necnon vinea vera
   Ex Aegypto transducta.

5. Certe civitas firma,
   Fortis, atque unita,
   Gloriosa, ac digna,
   Supra montem posita.

6. Arca Cherubin tecta,
   Omni parte aurata,
   Sacrosanctis reperta,
   Viris quatuor portata.

7. Christo regina apta,
   Solis luce amicta,
   Simplex, simulque docta,
   Undecumque invicta.

8. Vere regalis aula,
   Variis gemmis ornata,
   Gregisque Christe caula
   Patre summo servata.

9. Virgo valde fecunda
   Haec, et mater intacta,
   Laeta ac tremebunda,
   Verbo dei subacta.

10. Cui vita beata
  Cum perfectis futura,
  Deo Patre parata
  Sine fide mansura.

  Benchuir bona regula.

AB II, p. 28; RCLP, pp. 69-70

All ten quatrains display a regular and patterned dissyllabic and trisyllabic accentual end-rime, usually perfect in terms of the Irish rules (except in quatrain 7, where *apta docta* consonate; and in quatrains 2 and 6, where *ct* and *rt* give questionable consonance). Both pairs of alternate lines within the quatrain are joined by end-rime. Every one of the forty lines of the poem is linked to its adjacent lines by a characteristic device. Within the line alliteration, assonance and consonance are frequent. Every line of the poem ends with the letter *a*: monorime is combined with changing accentual rime.

With so much emphasis on the end-links, it was perhaps inevitable that the poet should have employed more tenuous links between the close of one line and the beginning of the next. Though all the quatrains are linked, alliteration is the device in but four of the nine links: 1-2, *m;* 6-7, *qu ch;* 7-8, *v;* 8-9, *v.* Assonance. which is sometimes a rather slight device, occurs frequently as a link, although consonance is the device most often used for linking adjacent lines in the poem, aside from the invariable end-assonance. An analysis confined to representative quatrains will suffice to illustrate the usage of the poem with regard to ornament and links:

Intralinear Ornament	*Devices*
*N*avis *n*umquam turb*ata*,	alliteration, assonance
Quam*vis* flucti*bus* tonsa,	consonance
*N*up*ti*is qu*oque* par*ata*	consonance
Regi d*om*ino spo*n*sa.	consonance
*D*omus *d*eliciis plena,	alliteration
Su*per petra*m cons*tr*uc*ta*,	consonance, assonance
Necnon *vi*nea *ve*ra	alliteration, consonance
Ex Aegypto trans*ducta*.	alliteration, consonance

Intralinear Ornament	*Devices*
*C*erte *c*ivitas firm*a*,	alliteration, assonance
*F*ortis, *atque unita*,	alliteration, consonance
*G*loriosa, *ac* di*gna*,	assonance
*Su*pra *m*onte*m* posi*ta*.	consonance, assonance

Interlinear Links	*Lines*	*Devices*
Na*v*is num*quam* turba*ta*,		
Quamvis flu*cti*bu*s* tonsa,	1–2	entrance rime, consonance, assonance
*N*uptiis quoque parata	2–3	consonance
*R*egi domino sp*onsa*.	3–4	alliteration
	4–1	consonance
*Dom*us deliciis *plena*,		
Super p*etram* construct*a*,	1–2	consonance
*N*ecno*n* vine*a* vera	2–3	rime, assonance
*E*x Aegypto transd*ucta*.	3–4	assonance
	4–1	consonance
Certe civ*itas* firm*a*,		
*F*ortis, atque unit*a*,	1–2	alliteration, consonance
*G*loriosa, ac d*igna*,	2–3	assonance, entrance consonance
*S*upra montem posita.	3–4	consonance, assonance

The amount of assonance is somewhat obscured by the extent to which assonance is present in devices that qualify as consonance; for example, *plena* and *petram* are better assonances than consonances, though they do consonate roughly; again, *sponsa* and *domus* assonate on *o*, though they also consonate. Notice also the tendency to find links between other than contiguous words— probably in consequence of the use of such rich rime.

The style of a number of the surviving Hiberno-Latin hymns is better typified by a Hymn to the Virgin attributed to St Cuchuimne than by any of the poems so far analysed. In this hymn, for interlinear linkage at points other than verse-ends, rime serves equally with alliteration; and both assonance and consonance serve more frequently than rime and alliteration. Notice also the tendency of end-rime to force a linkage of parallel rather than contiguous elements of adjacent lines. The first four stanzas (of thirteen) illustrate the salient traits of the technique:

Cantemus in omni die/concinentes uarie
conclamantes deo dignum/ymnum sanctae Mariae

Bis per chorum hinc et inde/collaudemus Mariam
ut uox pulset omnem aurem/per laudem uicariam

Maria de tribu Iudae/summi mater domini
oportunam dedit curam/egrotanti homini

Gabriel aduexit uerbum/sinu prius paterno
quod conceptum et susceptum/in utero materno

LH I, p. 33

The end-rime is regularly trisyllabic and accentual throughout.
Notice the entrance consonance linking the first three lines of the
opening quatrain, and the link of internal rime between the third
and fourth lines (*dignum, ymnum*). Assonance becomes increasingly
the typical intralinear ornament; for example, the first quatrain:
i in the first line, *e* in the second, *ae* in the fourth. The quatrains
quoted also exemplify two common principles of Old and Middle
Irish verse ornament: the second couplet of the quatrain should be
the more ornately graced, as in the first two quatrains above.
The presence of inlaid rime in the first line of a couplet lifts the
requirement of a strong link between the lines of the couplet, as
in the second couplet of the third and fourth quatrains above. In
nine of the thirteen stanzas of the hymn, the end word of the third
line rimes with a word internal to the fourth. In the other four
stanzas, dissyllabic rime occurs in the third line at the third and
fourth, and seventh and eighth syllables, thus dividing the line in two.

In both stanzaic structure and ornament, the hymn to St Michael
attributed to St Colman McMurchon is similar to, but not identical
with, St Cuchuimne's *Hymn to the Virgin*. The first three stanzas
of the eleven stanza piece illustrate the salient traits:

In trinitate spes mea/fixa non in omine
et archangelum deprecor/Michaelem nomine

Ut sit obuius ac misus/mihi deo doctore
hora exitus de uita/ista atque corpore

Ne me ducat in amarum/minister inergiae
ipse princeps tenebrarum/atque pes superbiae

LH I, p. 44

The end-rime is regularly trisyllabic and accentual throughout. All adjacent lines and all quatrains are interlinked. The linkage between the end of one line and the beginning of the next tends to be more tenuous than in the other poems analysed. Alliteration, consonance and assonance are used for this linkage with almost equal frequency. Intralinear ornament depends primarily on alliteration but also on consonance and, slightly less often, on assonance. The poem is not nearly so rich in internal rimes as the poems attributed to St Oengus mac Tipraite and St Cuchuimne.

To recapitulate: The Hiberno-Latin poetry which appears to date from the fifth and sixth centuries exhibits a style of verse ornament substantially identical with that of Ambrose and Sedulius. This ornament is neither accentual nor phonetically classed: it may reflect characteristics of a popular verse presumably current in the Latin vernaculars of Gaul and Britain. Hiberno-Latin poetry which appears to date from the middle of the sixth to the middle of the seventh century exhibits systematic, non-accentual end-rime. Hiberno-Latin poetry embodying the full ornament of Old Irish verse cannot be established as of earlier composition than the late seventh century.[17] *Versiculi Familiae Benchuir*, which was certainly composed by 691, could be older—but by how many years it is impossible to determine. St Colman Mac Murchon, to whom is attributed the Hiberno-Latin Hymn in Praise of St Michael analysed above, is probably the Colman Mac Murchon whose obit is recorded by the *Four Masters* at the year 731. St Oengus mac Tipraite, to whom is attributed the Hymn to St Martin analysed above, died, according to the *Annals of Ulster*, in 745. St Cuchuimne, supposed author of the Hymn to the Virgin analysed above, died, according to the *Annals of Ulster*, in 746. Cuchuimne's hymn appears in manuscripts of German provenance (but probably Irish authorship) dating from the eighth, ninth and tenth centuries. Colman Mac Murchon's hymn appears in a ninth-century manuscript of German provenance; and the hymn is apparently referred to in the *Book of Mulling*, another ninth-century manuscript. Thus, the scholiastic attributions in the *Liber Hymnorum*, so far as they relate to time of authorship, are consistent with the testimony of other documents.

As has been observed from the masterpieces of Hiberno-Latin verse examined above, the application of Old Irish prosody to Latin offered no insurmountable difficulty, though it entailed significant adjustments. Less rich than Old Irish in the variety of consonants, consonant combinations and vowel combinations, Latin nevertheless provides greater opportunity for the use of assonance within the verse unit, because Latin is highly inflectional, with a profusion of conjugational and declensional terminations whose sounds are often similar or identical. In adapting their accentual alliteration to Latin, Irish poets were often forced to find an alliterative correspondence in the interior of a Latin word, since in so many Latin trisyllables and polysyllables the chief stress does not fall on the first or even the second syllable. Further, the syllabic length of the words paired in accentual end-rime cannot be so strictly regulated in Latin as in Irish, because so many Latin words are not accented on the first syllable.

The adjustments necessitated by application of the Old Irish system of ornament to Latin verse are evidence that the Old Irish system does not derive from Latin usage, but the reverse. If the system had been derived from Latin, would it have required adaptation when applied to the language of its source?

To conclude, the Hiberno-Latin poems disclose a development in verse ornament from the 'Ambrosian' to the Old Irish style. This development is an historical process covering almost three centuries. The chronology of this development supports a thesis: not the derivation of Old Irish ornament from Latin rhetoric, but rather the derivation of Hiberno-Latin ornament from Old Irish.

7

Derivation

It may be taken as the basic law of Celtic prosody that ornament derives from structure, and structure from stress. The derivation of structure from stress is apparent from Part I of this study. The derivation of ornament from structure becomes apparent from our exposition in Part II.

Alliteration

Substantial affinities exist between early Celtic (Irish, Welsh) and early Germanic alliteration. Atkinson and Kuno Meyer had early concluded (with Bergin later concurring) that the rules of Irish alliteration reflected a prehistoric linguistic condition before initial sounds had been affected by lenition or nasalization,[18] Comparative analysis of Celtic and Germanic alliteration indicates that the Celts and Germans early shared a community of alliterative technique, that the Celts probably regularized this technique, and that Old Irish alliteration (and certain other Old Irish and Old Welsh devices) evolved organically from a form of verse substantially identical with the oldest Germanic poetry. This poetry exhibits not only an alliterative style in some ways identical with that of the oldest Celtic verse, but also characteristics that seem to be preconditions for the development of distinctive traits of early Irish and Welsh verse technique—and certainly of the link or chain alliteration that distinguishes some of the oldest surviving Irish verse.[19]

Thus, in Germanic verse, the use of an alliterative link between the end of one verse unit and the beginning of the next is not uncommon *within the long verse*.[20] This fact is illustrated by the alliterative patterns *aa/ax* and *xa/aa*, and especially by the pattern *ab/ba*, in which there is no correspondence whatsoever between alternate positions in the *alliterative accentual* scheme.

thū biguolen *S*inthgunt, *S*unna, era *s*wister

xa/aa HDV I, p. 102

than *th*orrot thiu *th*iod thurh that ge*th*wing mikil

$$\text{aa/ax} \quad \text{HDV I, p. 98}$$

*L*ūcas endi *J*ōhannes, sia wārun *g*ode *l*ieba

$$\text{ab/ba} \quad \text{HDV I, p. 104}$$

Again, some specimens of early Germanic verse exhibit a systematic sense-carryover from the second half of one long verse to the first half of the next. In alliterative verse, such systematization of sense-carryover is the likely preliminary to a corresponding systematization of sound. Within the unitary Germanic long verse, this systematized correspondence of sense and sound is the most salient trait. But in Germanic poetry, this correspondence does not extend beyond the long verse. Sometimes, indeed, consecutive long verses alliterate on an identical sound; but there is no sustained chain of alliteration in the Irish manner. In Old Irish verse, however, the principle of a correspondence between sound and sense was utilized to create a continuous chain of alliterative links between the end of one verse unit and the beginning of the next.

It is clear, then, that Old Irish chain alliteration could very well have originated from a conscious utilization of certain verse elements characteristic of surviving early Germanic verse and of a (presumed) strictly comparable early Celtic verse. Usage of the alliterative pattern *ab/ba* within the long verse, and the effort to achieve a continuous correspondence of sense and sound, must have led Celtic poets to the alliterative pattern *ab/bc, cd/de*, etc.

Though *binding* alliteration had become a traditional device by the Old Irish period, specimens of Old Irish verse have survived that embody an early form of this *binding*—the device of *conachlonn*, whereby the last word of one line is repeated as the first word of the next, thus achieving a strict (if rudimentary) correspondence between sense-carryover and sound-carryover. *Binding* by name repetition would obviously have occurred in primitive genealogical poems, comparably to the Biblical strings of 'begats'. Rudimentary name and word linkage may well have been the precipitant that first suggested alliterative linkage.

Technically, Old Irish alliteration is an advance over Germanic *Stabreim*. This being so, it seems fairly obvious that Goidelic poets adopted chain alliterations as an element of verse style at some time after the cessation of intimate Goidelic-Germanic relations—not necessarily, though quite possibly, after the Goidelic migration to Ireland. The adoption or discovery of chain alliteration by the Goidels would likely have affected Germanic verse if this adoption had occurred during the early period of Goidelic-Germanic intimacy.

The question remains whether the Celtic-Germanic community of alliterative technique reflects a parallel development from an hypothetical Aryan source or an influence exercised by Celts on Germans or the reverse. At this time, only general considerations can be offered toward a decision as to the original source of the elements common to Celtic and Germanic alliteration:

- The Celts exploited alliteration more completely than the Germans.
- Old Irish alliteration is an advance beyond early Germanic in structural technique.
- Early Celtic design in metalwork etc. is superior to early Germanic in structural technique.

These general considerations—though by no means conclusive— suggest that the early Celts imparted more to the early Germans, in the matter of alliteration, than they received. In any event, Celtic-Germanic alliteration doubtless began as a sporadic ornament, whose application became increasingly frequent and increasingly conscious as the structure of the prehistoric verse became increasingly regular under the impulsion of vocal stress.

Rime, Consonance, Assonance

Old Irish rime, consonance and assonance have the same phonetic basis, whether these ornaments occur compulsorily as in the *riming stanzaic* verse, or frequently yet sporadically as in the *shamanistic* verse, or occasionally as in the *alliterative accentual* verse. The set incidence of ornament in various of the more complex forms of *riming stanzaic* verse is a structural and stylistic feature ultimately explicable in terms of the evolution of Celtic verse forms. The ornament is the same in kind, however, in *shamanistic* verse. In this verse, whose structure depends on repetition of grammatical patterns, the derivation of ornament from structure is readily apparent, because the grammatical parallelism is consistently reinforced by a parallelsim of ornament—of alliteration, assonance, consonance and rime (including entrance-rime, internal rime, interlaced rime, inlaid rime and end-rime).

Some forms of rime and consonance occur sporadically within the *alliterative accentual* verse line. Early Celtic intralinear rime and consonance were substantially identical with early Germanic forms of these ornaments, and were an organic consequence of the common principle underlying early Celtic-Germanic alliteration. This alliteration coincides with the accentual structure of the verse it ornaments, through correspondences between the initial elements of accented syllables and sound complexes. So far as early Celtic and Germanic intralinear rime and consonance consist in types employed mutually, such types occur at the precise accentual positions where alliteration is normally compulsory:

Éo *Ró*ssa, *ró*th *rú*irech,	ab/bc		
*ré*cht *f*látha, *fū*aimm *tú*inne . . .	cd/de	MPIM,	p. 2

*Do*ss *dāi*le *dā*l *T*emro,	ab/bc		
*to*ccad *cāi*n *cōe*m*n*ae *cō*ecat blīadnae . . .			
	cd/de	MAID, II,	p. 15

*Sō*ër *cathm*īl *coem*fata *M*ōen *L*a*b*raid *L*o*ṅg*sech			
	abb/bcc		
*l*eo *nī*thach, *n*athchobir, *c*athchobir *com*sech			
	cdd/de	MAID I,	pp. 16–17

*bē*n zi *bē*na, *bl*uot zi *bl*uoda	aa/aa	HDV I,	p. 103

thū biguolen *S*i*n*thgunt, *S*u*nn*a, era swister			
	xa/aa	HDV I,	p. 102

*sp*enis mih mit dīnēm *w*ortun, wili mih dīnu *sp*eru *w*e*r*pan			
	ab/ab	HDV I,	p. 103

Since the patterns of alliteration indicated by these illustrations are basic in Celtic and Germanic alliterative verse, the intralinear rime and consonance in the illustrations may hence be regarded as founded on extensions of the principle by which Celtic-Germanic alliteration was applied. However, whereas the alliteration consists in correspondences of the initial elements of sound complexes, the kinds of intralinear rime and consonance illustrated here consist in correspondences of entire syllables and sound complexes.

The question here arises as to whether the Celts or the Germans first developed intralinear rime and consonance. The oldest surviving poetry of both peoples employs such ornaments—but the Celtic poetry does so systematically, and the Germanic sporadically. Despite subsequent divergence the Celts and Germans evidently once employed a verse of substantially identical structure so far as the placement of alliteration was concerned. The same, therefore, must once have been true also of the intralinear rime and consonance —especially as rudimentary forms of these ornaments are, in some measure, statistically inevitable concomitants of Celtic-Germanic alliterative technique. Both in the ornaments and in alliteration the Celts progressed beyond the Germans, as far as complexity, variety and system are concerned, in the centuries following the decline of the early Celtic-Germanic intimacy on the continent. What evidence there is thus tends to suggest that the Celts first regularized the technique of Celtic-Germanic intralinear rime and consonance.

Intralinear consonance appears in its simplest form, correspondence of identical consonants without regard to vowels, in Welsh and Irish *cynghanedd*. This ornament remained optional in Irish verse, so far as available specimens reveal; in Welsh, it became a compulsory feature of certain forms but not, however, until the Middle Welsh period.

So long as the Celts did not discriminate in vowel colour, as in their alliteration, there could be no distinction of consonance from rime. Hence Celtic-Germanic intralinear consonance may be regarded as a precursor of rime. Rime began to exist as such for the Celts when, in their use of consonance, they began to discriminate in vowel colour for the purposes of poetic ornament.

Can one account for the unique phonetic basis of Old Irish consonance and rime in terms of antecedent circumstances?

Accentual rime and consonance are ornaments whose recognition necessarily involves the recognition of syllables as such. These ornaments are intrinsically syllabic.

The recognition of syllables is typically a consequence of linguistic study. This circumstance leads to speculations regarding the precise content of the early Gaulish and Irish literary curricula.

What was it that was studied in Gaul and in Ireland under the druid as high poet for up to twenty years?

The ogham inscriptions testify to the existence and use, well into the Old Irish period, of proto-Goidelic, an archaic form of Irish, highly inflectional in comparison with the Old Irish vernacular, and related to this vernacular much as Classical Latin is related to the early state of Romance languages. This proto-Goidelic persisted as the language of the old religion, of the druidism that preceded, and for centuries co-existed with, Irish Christianity.

Druidic lore and language were preserved orally and taught in secret. The oral transmission of an archaic tongue leads inevitably to an awareness of grammar, including phonetics. The preservation of the Hindu Vedas, under comparable circumstances, led to an elaborate development of Sanskrit grammar. Very likely, the phonetic basis of Old Irish rime, consonance and assonance derives ultimately from druidic efforts to impart a knowledge of, and thus to preserve, the ritual, liturgy and myth of the religion and culture that Christianity eventually superseded.

Proto-Goidelic was a highly inflected language, with case endings and (no doubt) declensional forms comparable to those of other Indo-European languages at the same stage of linguistic development. In consequence, many adjoining verse lines in proto-Goidelic would terminate in speech complexes often involving a number of similarly sounding syllables. *Shamanistic* verse in proto-Goidelic, based as it must have been on the repetition of grammatical patterns, would have been particularly rich in aural correspondences throughout the verse line, correspondences often obtained without contrivance, as in the earliest Hiberno-Latin hymns.

The progressive loss of suffixes and the rise of initial inflection in the vernacular that succeeded proto-Goidelic, together with the survival of verse rich in such endings in the sacred language of Celtic paganism, must have presented a continuously effective spur to poets using the vernacular, and would have motivated them to achieve correspondences, at salient points of the verse unit, as rich comparably as those of the sacred language. These salient points, because of the linguistic change, would be root syllables—increasingly, final syllables—bearing a strong speech stress.

Such impetus, coupled with the increasing awareness of the phonetic distinctions and syllabification that necessarily attended transmission of the archaic tongue, would have encouraged the systematic use of rich end-ornament in vernacular poetry—end-ornament that would not supplant the alliterative technique of proto-Goidelic and the use of consonance, but that would refine the consonance by regulating it according to the 'new' phonetics and that would add assonance (correspondence of vowels by colour) to the consonance, thus creating systematic rime.

To the extent that poets who were learned in the archaic tongue created verse also in the vernacular, the impulse to enrich the vernacular would be capable of ready realization. The *filid* or learned poets were, however, a class distinct from (and far more privileged than) the bards or minstrels, who depended primarily on the people for sustenance. Hence, the impulse to ornament the vernacular would not necessarily have been felt most keenly by the class of poets best able to enrich and to systematize the verse of the people. But that the learned poets eventually applied their art to such verse is indicated by the fact that, though the bards were considered in early Irish law as not legally entitled to payment for their product, their more complex stanzaic forms were actually the subject of study by the *filid* at a certain point in the literary curriculum—and the *filid* were definitely entitled to payment for what they might produce in the bardic forms.

Possessed, then, of phonetics beyond that of traditional Celtic alliteration, as well as of an interest in exploiting their knowledge, the learned poets would be inclined to utilize phonetics where they could; and this would be in the regulation of verse ornaments that so far had been used only sporadically in the alliterative verse— ornaments in which the whole syllable, rather than only its initial sounds, would be engaged; that is, the ornaments of consonance, assonance and rime. Consonance in Celtic verse also became assonance, once the vowels were classed as *a*, *o*, *u* and *e*, *i*; and rime, once identical vowels were used systematically at corresponding stresses.

It should not be supposed that assonance and even rime were unobserved phenomena before the advent of the 'new' phonetics. Their sporadic incidence was statistically inevitable in a language rich in inflectional endings. Their frequent occurrence was inevitable in verse that relied for effect on the reiteration of a grammatical pattern. A question remains only as to the period when ornament was first systematized according to the 'new' phonetics, wedded to stress accent and made compulsory at set places in the verse structure.

The emergence of Old Irish as the spoken tongue among all social classes, and the consequent reservation of proto-Goidelic to the purposes of druidry, likely motivated the learned poets to compose verse in the vernacular, whether by modernizing earlier styles or by systematizing and complicating the bardic measures. The sheer economics of the language shift would have forced the learned poets to utilize the emerging vernacular. Their superior knowledge of phonetics, their skill in all forms of verse, their legal privileges and their traditional prestige (as prophet, diviner and magician) would have enabled them to keep ahead of the bard or the folk minstrel.

But when did Old Irish emerge as the spoken tongue for all classes?

Proto-Goidelic survives chiefly if not entirely in the ogham inscriptions on memorial stones, found principally in southern Ireland and also in southwest Wales. These inscriptions overlap chronologically the beginnings (in the sixth century AD) of Old Irish documentation. Proto-Goidelic was doubtless archaic for centuries earlier, since Old Irish—from the beginning of its documentation—had already shed the inflectional endings that distinguish proto-Goidelic, and stood toward the archaic tongue as Old French to Classical Latin.

Given the accepted facts of archaeology and history, the Goidels entered Ireland during (and probably to some extent before and after) the Age of Caesar. These Goidels brought with them a language at least as highly inflected as the Gaulish of Caesar's time—a level of inflection fairly represented by the language of the ogham inscriptions. It is likely that the loss of inflections from proto-Goidelic was hastened by a language difference between the invading Goidels and their predecessors in Ireland—some of them p-Celts, some of them non-Celtic aborigines. These conquered peoples were reduced in status, possessions and numbers, but were not exterminated. Hence, the Goidelic development of the 'new' phonetics, from the necessity of teaching an archaic sacred language, must have become a pressing requirement within a century or two after Caesar.

But the circumstances that prompted the 'new' phonetics would also have prompted its application to the ornament of vernacular verse. The basic rules of Old Irish rime, consonance, and assonance, and their application by the *filid* to verse forms previously proper to the bards, consequently would antedate the beginning of Hiberno-Latin literature by some centuries.

It is consistent with the findings of comparative analysis that Old Irish prosodic tracts should exist, containing extensive terminology relative to the structure and ornament of Old Irish verse, and that no prosodic tracts should exist pertaining to Hiberno-Latin verse.[21] Further, the terminology used in the Old Irish tracts is not Latin-derived, but forms an indigenous vocabulary. Scholiastic comments in eleventh-century manuscripts, pertaining to various Hiberno-Latin poems, employ a few common terms from the prosody of mediaeval Continental Latin, but disclose no terms that pertain to the distinguishing Irish features of the poems, despite the fact that certain of the poems display the full system of Old Irish ornament. The monastic scholiasts make no prosodic comments on the Old Irish *riming stanzaic* verse contained in the same eleventh-century sources.

Scholiastic chronology supports the findings of comparative analysis: the probable date of *Brigit be bithmaith*, based on scholiastic attributions, is anterior to the probable dates of Hiberno-Latin verse using the same system of ornament as *Brigit be bithmaith*, based on scholiastic attributions also; and these are consistent with other evidence.

The glosses on *Amra Choluimb Chille* attribute various traits of the poem to its emulation of pagan verse. The poem itself contains what may be a vaunt of its success in such emulation. The penultimate line of the composition, praising the poem, is revealing: 'Vast the variation, vast, as of a poem in praise of heaven's holy lights.' The glosses on this line interpret it as follows: 'great is the exceeding variation (from ordinary language) which I have put upon these words above', and 'great is the poem which the poets at first used to make to the sun and to the moon, and not greater was the darkening they used to put upon them than I have put here.' (BACC, p. 419) Whatever the poem to the sun and the moon was really like, it must have been a pagan composition, and perhaps a phase of worship. Further, this poem was composed in a language 'vastly' at variance with the colloquial; and *Amra*

Choluimb Chille is written in a language supposedly inspired by, though not necessarily copied from, the language of the pagan poem. The poet who wrought the language of both *Amra Choluimb Chille* and *Amra Senain* sought to outdo the druids.

But what view prevailed in Old Irish times as to the origin of rime ? Though the extensive early Irish prosodic and grammatical tracts contain no hint that Irish rime derived from Latin, one of these tracts attributes the invention of rime to a pagan Irish poet-king—*Lugair-lanfili*.

Summary

The indigenous origin of Old Irish verse ornament is an hypothesis justifiable by its utility in correlating all the available facts and circumstances pertinent to this ornament. We have of course broadened the spectrum of fact and circumstance by noticing prosodic traits and even poems often overlooked, and by analyzing verse ornament with more rigour than supports previous studies. But the point of view is not entirely novel: our analyses implement the judgements of earlier men (Zeuss, O'Curry, Hyde) who had not the occasion to develop detailed hypotheses. If our concepts should betoken a revolutionary turn, the revolution is rather a restoration and extension of positions held by the founders of Celtic philology. Yet, even as we reject concepts advanced by such eminent Celticists of an earlier generation as Thurneysen and Kuno Meyer, we praise their editorial diligence in bringing before the scholarly world those manuscripts whose contents incidentally permit of the analyses controverting certain theories: that of the Latin derivation of Old Irish verse ornament, and that of the Latin derivation of Old Irish stanzaic forms.

We have summarized the rules of early Celtic verse ornament and shown their incidence relative to the gamut of early Celtic verse, so as to document the early and general use of the ornament, and clarify its vast differences from the proffered Latin sources. The evolution of Hiberno-Latin verse ornament, as we sketched it, shows a gradual approach to the system of ornament that already existed, fully matured, in Old Irish verse. The gradual character of this approach supports a corollary to the concept of indigenous origin; namely, the derivation of Hiberno-Latin ornament from the Old Irish. Our discussion of the derivation of Old Irish ornament, reflecting close comparative analysis, leads us to the threshold of Indo-European archetypes.

In conclusion:

1. Old Irish verse ornament is phonetic and accentual in principle, and uniquely systematic in application.

2. Its vast differences, in principle and application, from the ornament of Late Latin 'rimed prose' preclude its derivation from this prose.

3. It appears as a matured system in all the forms and in the earliest available states of Old Irish poetry.

4. It is the source of the final style of Hiberno-Latin verse ornament and the inspiration of its transitional styles.

5. It derives from an indigenous Celtic phonetics and from Celtic-Germanic verse of prehistoric, possibly Indo-European, origin.

6. Old Irish rime and its variants became systematically accentual and phonetic during some period between the first and sixth centuries AD.

Part III : Theories of Latin Derivation

Introduction

Theories of Latin derivation for Celtic verse forms and ornament are in effect controverted by the evidence of their indigenous origin, adduced in Parts I and II, above. It remains to refute formally such theories still held as to Irish verse, by the elucidation of their terms and by the specification of their incompatibility with fact and right reason. We pass over, however, the comparable notions of Rhys as to Welsh verse, inasmuch as they never met with considered acceptance.

Thurneysen early proposed the derivation of Old Irish stanzaic form from Latin hymns. (TIAV, pp. 309–47)   Wilhelm Meyer (Speyer) maintained that Old Irish verse ornament derived from Late Latin 'rimed prose'.[1]   Polheim (PLRP) and Kuno Meyer took substantially the same view, though on divergent grounds. Zimmer also endorsed the concept.[2]   Although Zeuss, the founder of Celtic philology, took for granted the indigenous origin of Celtic verse forms and ornament, the prestige of concepts launched subsequently by certain of the second generation of German Celticists has survived both the strenuous objections of the poet-scholar Sigerson (whose ardour exceeded his analytic flair),[3] and the reservations of Douglas Hyde. (HLHI)   As recently as 1961, Gerard Murphy affirmed the Latin derivation of Irish rime and stanza, invoking primarily the speculations of Wilhelm Meyer and Polheim as to ornament and of Thurneysen as to stanzaic forms. (MEIM)

The various concepts of Latin derivation are not compatible with one another. It was necessary to Thurneysen's case that the Irish poets should be granted to have practiced the use of accentual rime before their acquaintance with Latin hymns; but according to Wilhelm Meyer and Polheim, the Irish derived their rime from an acquaintance with Patristic 'rimed prose', after their conversion. Thurneysen rejected Wilhelm Meyer's assertion of a Latin derivation for the alliterative ornament of Irish *alliterative accentual* verse. Kuno Meyer tried to account for the elaborate early development of Irish verse ornament by assembling what evidence he could gather for a flight of Gaulish scholars to Ireland before the advent of Patrick. (LITL)

Of course the entire effort to derive Old Irish verse form and ornament from Latin verse or prose fails to take account not merely of such evidence as we have adduced but of a circumstance whose significance seems to have been overlooked by the scholars affected; namely, that both the Welsh and the Irish were early exposed to Latin 'rimed prose' and Latin hymns. Inasmuch as the character of early Irish Christianity reflects that of early Wales, it would seem inevitable that verse in Welsh should reflect Latin influence in much the same way as verse in Irish is alleged to have done. Instead, the few scraps of early Cambro-Latin verse reflect the usage of the earliest Welsh verse without closely approaching its refinements, just as the earliest Hiberno-Latin verse discloses a very gradual approach to the distinctive traits of Old Irish verse.

8

Structure

One of Thurneysen's earliest contributions to Celtic studies was his theory of the Latin derivation of the Irish 'syllabic' stanzas. (TIAV) Perhaps Ebel, in his editing of Zeuss, had supplied the hint. Thurneysen subsequently edited abundant material (some by 1891) from which a controversion of his theory might have been readily effected.

According to Thurneysen's theory, the *ymnum dicat* attributed to St Hilary of Poitiers is the seed from which Old Irish 'syllabic' stanzas ultimately derive:

Ymnum dicat turba fratrum ymnum cantus personet
Christo regi concinentes laudem demus debitam[4]

LH, I, p. 36

Audite omnes amantes
Deum sancta merita
Viri in Christo beati
Patricii episcopi   AB, II, p. 14

Thurneysen assumed that *audite omnes amantes*, attributed to St Sechnall, was modelled on *ymnum dicat*, save that quantity was ignored. Sechnall's rendering of trochaic tetrameter would thus be one of those fruitful misunderstandings not unknown in the history of art. Though quantity was disregarded, the quantitative pattern did not become a rhythmic pattern; rather, the syllabic measure of the verse units became the norm. Syllabic measure, an irrelevancy and an automatic by-product in learned Latin verse, becomes in *audite omnes amantes* the basis of Irish stanzaic verse in both Latin and the vernacular. But this is not all. The verse-ends in 'Hilary's hymn' and in *audite omnes amantes* are fairly regular in rhythm. Irish imitators, observing this, produced syllabic measures with regular rhythmic cadence.

The circumstance that *ymnum dicat* is preserved only in Irish manuscripts and that it differs radically in prosody from the indisputably genuine fragments of Hilary's verse has caused no-one to declare that the hymn might be an Irish or an insular composition. Wilhelm Meyer, nevertheless, assigned it to a later Hilary than Hilary of Poitiers.[5] Apparently the regard for quantity has been taken to indicate that the hymn was not of Irish authorship, despite the fact that Columbanus, by the early seventh century, wrote competent quantitative verse in Latin. (RSLP, I, pp. 162–64) The attribution to Hilary of Poitiers of a hymn in an Irish manuscript (*Antiphonary of Bangor*) dating from the late seventh century has the less weight considering that an Hiberno-Latin hymn in the same manuscript bears an attribution (albeit qualified) to the apostles! It is at once evident that Thurneysen's theory rests on an enormous assumption. (One sees of course that *audite omnes amantes* differs considerably from *ymnum dicat* in stress rhythm. *Ymnum dicat* is trochaic tetrameter in stress as well as quantity. *Audite omnes amantes* approaches the quite different rhythm of the Celtic verse foot. Further, the evidence of its sixth-century forgery plays havoc with Thurneysen's assumptions.)

According to Thurneysen, the addition of accentual end-rime to stanzas like Hilary's and Sechnall's on the part of the writers of Hiberno-Latin hymns led to the establishment of the Irish verse measures *Seadna Mór* and *Seadna*:[6]

Seadna Mór: $8^2 + 7^3$ 12345678   1234567
(alternate dissyllabic and trisyllabic verse-ends)

Seadna: $8^2 + 7^1$ 12345678   1234567
(alternate dissyllabic and monosyllabic verse-ends)

These measures arose through Irish imitation in the vernacular of such hymns as those by St Cuchuimne and St Colman Mac Murchon:

> Cantemus in omni die concinentes uarie
> conclamantes deo dignum ymnum sanctae Mariae
>
> > *Cuchuimne*, LH, I, p. 33

> In trinitate spes mea fixa non in omine
> et archangelum deprecor Michaelem nomine
>
> > *Mac Murchon*, LH, I, p. 44

That is, Irish poets systematized the regular rhythm which characterized the verse-ends of the Hiberno-Latin imitations of Hilary; and then the vernacular poets made compulsory a dissyllabic rime-word for the close of the eight-syllable verse unit, and a trisyllabic rime-word for the close of the seven-syllable verse unit. This was the manner in which the verse structure termed *Seadna Mór* came into being. And *Seadna*? The character of the Irish language etc. made a monosyllabic verse-end inevitable, in the seven-syllable verse unit.

Other measures evolved through a shortening of the first half of the now regularized couplet to seven syllables:

Dian airseng: $7^1 + 7^3$ 1234567   1234567
Rannaigecht mór: $7^1 + 7^1$ 1234567   1234567

Still others evolved through a shift of accents arising from use of a dissyllabic and trisyllabic verse-end instead of a monosyllabic:

Rannaigecht bec: $7^2 + 7^2$ 1234567   1234567
Cas bairdne: $7^3 + 7^3$ 1234567   1234567

Then, a dropping of syllables in the second half of the couplet; and then in both halves:

Cro-cummaisc etir casbairdne ocus
lethrannaigecht: $7^3 + 5^1$ 1234567   12345
Lethrannaigecht mór: $5^1 + 5^1$ 12345   12345

Thurneysen does not offer Hiberno-Latin examples for most of the phases of the evolution just outlined—no Latin examples exist for each of even the handful of measures just listed. Indeed, there are *no* Latin hymns that fully conform with the measures *Seadna* and *Seadna mór*, which were supposedly immediately suggested by the syllabic and accentual structure of Latin hymns. The distinctively Irish features of Irish syllabic measures—the regularization of the syllabic length and accentual pattern of the verse-ends, and the patterned accentual rime—have no continental Latin prototype and none, so far as regulated verse-ends are concerned, even in surviving Hiberno-Latin hymns. Some of these hymns certainly *approach* regularity in the syllabic measure

*

of their verse-ends, but not before the late seventh and the early eighth centuries (as shown in Part II). If the scope of Thurneysen's theory should be confined to the evidence that can be advanced in its favour, the theory could not be said to show that Irish syllabic verse owed more to Latin hymns than perhaps the *idea* of syllabic measure and the *idea* of regularly rhythmical cadences: the actual character of Irish syllabic measures differs most significantly from that of Latin measures precisely at the verse-end—at the point where Latin influence was supposedly most fruitful. But Thurneysen's theory was controvertible with evidence accessible during his lifetime, some of it edited before he presented his theory, some of it edited by him not long after, and some of it edited by his fellow scholars. His theory can be summarized in four leading propositions:

- The Irish derived the syllabically regulated, accentually riming verse-ends of their quatrains from Latin hymns.
- The Irish derived the principle of syllabic regulation from Latin hymns.
- The Irish derived the quatrain as a form from Latin hymns.
- The Irish derived specific quatrains from Latin hymns.

The old Irish regulation of the accentually riming verse-end has three elements—rime, syllabic regulation of the verse-end and accentuation of the initial syllable of rime words. Old Irish verse of pagan background or incontestably native tradition contains all three elements, separately and in combination. Thus, in Old Irish, the speech accent usually fell on the first syllable—the root syllable. Further, we have already seen that accentual rime occurs in such Old Irish verse (pp. 53-58). Finally, syllabic regulation of the verse-end was a commonplace, regardless of the use or absence of rime. Certainly, the riming verse-ends in some of the sporadically riming verse of pagan background or incontestably native tradition are syllabically regulated: *chel sen* and *bebe febe* and *recht lecht fecht thecht* in the *Prayer for Long Life* (Part II, p. 57), *diclass digbas* in *Amorgen's Incantation* (Part I, p. 6), *luind tuind* in an excerpt from the *Táin Bó Cúalgne* (Part I, p. 8). The riming verse-ends in certain Old Irish non-syllabic quatrains are syllabically regulated:

Sithbacc lond,
Lugaid lūath,
loiscis trebthu
trēn tūath.

Cathach decheng
dāna fīal:
Fedelmid clothach
Corbmac ciar. MAID, I, p. 27

The verse-ends in unrimed or irregularly rimed verse are also often syllabically regulated. For example, the verse-ends are regularly dissyllabic in various specimens of what Kuno Meyer termed the ancient alliterative verse (*Fo-chén Cét*—Part I, p. 11; *Fo-chén Lábraid*—Part I, p. 11); they are regularly trisyllabic in other specimens (Part I, p. 10); and regularly monosyllabic in still others (Part I, p. 12). In short, the Irish borrowed from Latin hymns neither the principle of the syllabic regulation of the accentually riming verse-end nor the elements on which this principle is founded: the principle does not appear in Latin verse, but both the principle and its elements appear in Irish pagan as well as Irish Christian verse.

Those who composed Irish verse in the ancient alliterative tradition not only regulated the verse-end syllabically (that is, rhythmically) but extended the principle of regulation to all parts of the verse line, as shown in Part I (*Amorgen's Incantation, Amorgen's Hymn*: Crenaid brain, Mora maitne, Fo-chén Lábraid, Cetach conn, Labraid luam, etc.). Evidently in this verse, because of *word foot* and *word measure* regulation of the stress pattern, syllabic regularity is sometimes more rigorous than in the later Irish Christian verse. The Irish assuredly did not derive the principle of rhythmic regulation from Latin hymns.

Did the Irish regulate the quatrain before they became Christian? Did they employ the quatrain at all, in pagan days?

Ever since the appearance of Thurneysen's theory on the origin of the Irish syllabic measures, a tendency has existed to deny that Ireland knew the quatrain as a verse form before Ireland became Christian. The *alliterative accentual* verse is held to be the characteristically pagan form; and the syllabic quatrain, the characteristically

Christian. Nevertheless, the *alliterative accentual* verse has survived in quatrain form, as may be perceived on examining one of Kuno Meyer's last monographs, 'Über die älteste irische Dichtung'. Non-syllabic *alliterative accentual* quatrains are quoted on p. 10 (this one rimeless) and on p. 9 (this one with end-rime).   Kuno Meyer's monograph contains sufficient additional examples, some attributed in their source to specific pagan poets, to explode the notion that the Irish knew nothing of the quatrain before they became familiar with Latin hymns, and the curious fallacy of assuming that, since the Irish pagans practiced one kind of verse, they did not practice others.   Quatrains occur also in the archaic legal verse of Ireland, as Watkins points out (wiem, pp. 227–29, 236), together with verse lines whose syllabic count is uniform within the verse paragraph, and whose strophes sometimes contain a regular alternation of verse lines that differ uniformly in syllabic count. The quatrain is in fact one of the most universal, yet antique, verse forms. The Chinese *Shih King* contains poems which date from 500 BC, and a number of poems in the *Shih King* employ the four-line stanza—actually, a stanza written as four squares of four symbols (*word feet*) each.

Of the four basic stanza types observable in Old Irish metrical tracts, three types cannot be derived from Latin hymns within the terms of Thurneysen's theory: the *ochtfochlach* family of stanzas, the *debide* family of stanzas, and the *draignech* stanzas. Indeed, the *rinnard* stanzas (basically, four six-syllable lines with dissyllabic line-ends, which is a class within the *rannaigecht* type) cannot be derived by Thurneysen's method, as shown by Watkins. (wiem, p. 248).

The *ochtfochlach* stanza is typically a double quatrain, in which the first three lines of the quatrain rime only with themselves, but the last line of each pair of quatrains rimes with the other (*rat fiat* etc.—see Part I, p. 35 above).   The last lines of the quatrains are not doubled couplets. They derive from the triad with refrain (Part I, pp. 32-35). They cannot be derived by addition and subtraction from Hilary or Ambrose.[7]

The *debide* stanza is typically a quatrain made up of two couplets that rime by paired consecutive lines, with an accent on the riming syllable compulsory in but one of each pair of rime words. In *atchiu fer find* (Part I, p. 25)—an example of early, irregular *debide*— the accented rime word may appear in either the first or second of a pair of rime words, and the verse-ends are not syllabically regulated.

Although the rime is accentual in the manner common to Irish poetry, the poem cannot be derived from Latin hymns in terms of Thurneysen's theory, because its cadences are irregular, its verse-ends are not syllabically measured, and its rime occurs within rather than between couplets. Normally in *debide*, the cadences are regular and the verse-ends are syllabically measured; but Thurneysen's theory still cannot derive *debide* from Latin hymns.

The *draignech* stanzas are considered even by Murphy to derive probably from Irish accentual verse. They are obviously not regulated syllabically, and their line is longer than anything in Hiberno-Latin verse.

Certain general considerations vitiate Thurneysen's theory. Once the regulating principle was discovered, Irish syllabic verse forms, according to Thurneysen, came into being by subtraction (and addition?). Again, Irish quatrains are syllabically measured (no accentual basis) except that the verse-end is regulated more precisely as to accent than in any other verse. Here, then, is an accentual non-accentual verse in which the forms are generated by means of arithmetic!

Let us grant that Thurneysen's theory is inadequate in premises and in detail. Even so, could it not be that the Irish, though consciously utilizing all the elements of their 'syllabic' quatrains as we have them, did not actually evolve their 'syllabic' quatrains until certain Latin hymns had inspired the Irish to imitate the obvious syllabic regularity of these hymns? In other words, regardless of the details whereby Irish quatrains actually coalesced, must we not assume that Latin hymns were the catalytic agent which actually precipitated the fusion into a system of syllabic quatrains of all the elements of such a system, which we have shown to be present in the verse of the Irish pagans?

Under the circumstances—specifically, the existence of many stanzaic measures that cannot be shown by any theory to derive from Latin hymns or any other Latin verse or rhetorical composi-tions—it seems extremely unlikely that the creation of any of the 'syllabic' measures of Old Irish verse proceeded from a Latin inspiration, however indirect or occasional.

Why should Latin hymns be regarded as the indispensable catalyst? Syllabism in verse is not a unique phenomenon. It occurs in ancient Sanskrit. It has been a basic principle in Japanese verse for centuries. The so-called 'syllabic' measures are attributed in early Irish prosody and law tracts to the bards, not the saints. The bards were originally the popular poets, as distinguished from the *filid* or professional men of letters. The bards existed as a class in pre-Christian Gaul.

Possibly the syllabic framework of certain Old Irish measures was suggested by Latin verse ? Did the Irish, even though possessing a variety of measures, acquire others from the suggestion of Latin hymns ?

The mere fact that certain Irish quatrains have the same general syllabic dimensions as certain Latin quatrains means little in this connection, since the Latin measures are so normal, and the Irish so numerous. The measure of Sechnall's *Sancti venite* (Part II, p. 69), less common in Latin than the measures of 'Hilary's Hymn' and the Ambrosian verse, is employed in Hiberno-Latin poems but apparently not in Old Irish, except in occasional quatrains that occur in poems of no fixed stanza pattern. It is highly significant that no Old Irish poems imitate the style of Colum Cille's Latin poem *Altus Prosator*, or any other of the transitional styles of Hiberno-Latin verse.

The Irish names of measures are not taken from Latin. No prosodic innovations are ascribed in Old Irish sources to worthies of the Church. All the terms necessary to denote the distinguishing features of the syllabic measures are available in Irish words that show no trace of Latin origin, although certain Latin terms have been Hibernicized and used in grammatical and prosodic commentaries—a fact that has caused some confusion. Specifically, the scholiastic commentaries in the *Liber Hymnorum* reveal a thorough ignorance of Irish technique and prosodic terminology, but some familiarity with the terminology of continental Christian-Latin prosody. Thus, the distinction between *rhythmus artificialis* and *rhythmus vulgaris* is recognized, and the second declared to consist in equality of syllables and correspondence of quarter verses and half verses (as in *Altus Prosator*). The scholiasts found the limit of their perceptions in such terms as end-rime, equality of syllables, line and half-line, and *capitulum*. Such terms fail to comprehend the peculiarly Irish devices of so many of the hymns, both Latin and Old Irish, in the *Liber Hymnorum*. It is noteworthy that there are no scholiastic observations in this manuscript on the prosody of the hymns in the Irish language which it contains, although both surviving copies of the manuscript, neither being a copy of the other, contain similar remarks on the prosody of the Latin hymns. Certainly, the lack of familiarity with Irish prosody displayed in the prefaces and commentaries of the *Liber Hymnorum* is no argument for the Latin source of Irish syllabic measures.

To summarize regarding the Old Irish so-called 'syllabic' verse-measures:

- The distinguishing features of the Old Irish system of stanzaic forms—rhythmic (and hence syllabic) regulation of the verse-end, and accentual rime of the regulated verse-end—are not present in non-Celtic verse, though approximated in some specimens of Hiberno-Latin verse.

- Hiberno-Latin verse does not closely approximate the distinguishing features of Old Irish verse until the late seventh and early eighth centuries, judging from the probable chronology of surviving specimens.

- The commentaries of Irish clerical scholiasts, written later than these centuries, betray an ignorance of Old Irish prosody and a familiarity with the concepts of continental Latin prosody, which, however, the scholiasts misapply to certain Hiberno-Latin hymns modelled on Old Irish verse.

- Old Irish verse of the most elaborate character, in rhythmically regulated quatrains (whose syllabic structure is necessarily uniform) survives from the late sixth and early seventh centuries. Some of this verse is certainly Christian in matter; some, certainly not.

- Old Irish Christian poets utilized the technique of Irish verse pagan in background and native in tradition, and Irish Christians utilized prayers and spells completely pagan in content and psychology.

- All the elements of the Old Irish system of rhythmically regulated stanzas are present in the Irish verse of pagan background and native tradition, including the quatrain framework, accentual rime, and the principle of the rhythmic (and hence syllabic) regulation of both the verse-ends and the verse line.

- Early Irish prosody tracts disclose a terminology—of Celtic origin—that comprehends both the general and distinguishing features of Old Irish stanzaic verse.

● Irish prosodic and legal tracts, and other sources of comment, attribute no poetic innovations to saints, but identify the Old Irish so-called 'syllabic' measures as proper to the bards, who were a distinct class in Celtic society before the Roman conquest of Gaul.

● The theory of the Latin derivation of Irish stanzaic form, first fully enunciated by Thurneysen, though generally taken to show that the Irish adopted Latin measures, actually shows that the distinguishing features of the Irish measures are not realized in Latin verse and *attempts to show* that these features were derived from suggestions offered by the structure of Latin hymns. Thurneysen's theory not only fails to take account of the evidence summarized above, but cannot be made to provide a Latin origin for three of the four Old Irish stanza types, nor for some subspecies of the fourth type, even if the premises and dynamics of his theory were to be accepted as valid. (All four stanza types have been shown to derive from indigenous antecedents— Part I, pp. 22-41).

Under the influence of Thurneysen's theory, Gerard Murphy attributed the heptasyllabic line in certain archaic legal verse to an 'experiment' on the suggestion of Latin hymns (MEIM, p. 19). This grotesquerie is well pinioned by Watkins:

. . . the functional position of this heptasyllabic verse in Early Irish society; its greatest use is precisely in the most conservative section of Early Irish culture, the law. This heptasyllabic line, with its numerous variant forms, runs through the oldest strata of our legal texts; that it should be a seventh-century experiment on the model of the Latin hymns, is contradicted by everything we know about Irish law. When we observe that these verse-lines are the metrical vehicle of a legal doctrine uninfluenced by Roman law, civil or canon; when we observe that the older the stratum of these legal texts, the more frequent is this verse-form; when we observe finally that in this same archaic stratum of the laws, there are essentially *no* Latin loanwords; then it is evident that this heptasyllabic metre can under no circumstances be an 'experiment' modelled on, or even in any way influenced by, Christian Latin hymnic tradition. (WIEM, p. 220).

9

Ornament

Wilhelm Meyer 'discovered' that rime originated under Syriac auspices, and passed from eastern to western Christianity.[8] Authorities on Syriac dismiss his 'discovery'.

Meyer's theory of the Latin source of Old Irish verse ornament is not elaborately developed in the essay in which he presents it. The vernacular verse is scarcely noticed. Poems in Old Irish are not even quoted, on the enormous assumption that Old Irish so-called syllabic poetry derived from Hiberno-Latin poetry. Meyer quotes from Hiberno-Latin poems that contain alliteration, assonance, end-rime and internal rime; however, he shows little awareness of what is unique in the Irish usage of these ornaments. This quoting and some references to Latin 'rimed prose' constitute the essence of his 'demonstration'. The *Hisperica Famina* he regards as rimed prose; and the *Epitomes of Publius Virgilius Maro* as a serious work of sixth century Latin scholarship.

In support of Wilhelm Meyer: Polheim shows that the Irish scholar and poet St Columbanus (by the seventh century) was familiar with the devices of 'rimed prose'. (PLRP) Further, the Compendium or Encyclopedia of St Isidore of Seville, containing 'rimed prose', seems to have become known in Ireland shortly after its completion (about 635 AD). (PLRP, p. 292 etc.) Kuno Meyer, nevertheless, preferred to account for the elaborate early development of Irish literary device by reliance on a flight of Gaulish scholars. (LITL)

Nothing that can be demonstrated from either chronological or prosodic analysis of the actually surviving Irish and Hiberno-Latin verse requires us to accept a Latin origin for, or contribution to, Irish verse forms or ornament. Very serious objections confront the concept of a Latin source for Celtic verse ornament:

● The proponents of Latin origin have not observed that the unique ornaments of Old Irish verse appear in the vernacular, in both christian and secular poetry, before they appear in Hiberno-Latin literature of any kind (Part II).

109

● The very great differences between Old Irish verse and Late
Latin 'rimed prose', both in form and ornament, are ignored
by Wilhelm Meyer et al. Thurneysen cited some of these differences in rejecting the notion that Old Irish *alliterative accentual*
verse derives from 'rimed prose'.[9]

● Close analysis of Hiberno-Latin verse ornament (Part II) establishes that Hiberno-Latin only gradually, over a period
of three centuries, assimilated the system of verse ornament
that is embodied from the outset in Old Irish vernacular verse.

● Distinctively Celtic ornaments, being without analogue among
the ornaments of Greek and Latin literatures, could not have
been derived from them. Even the Celtic ornaments that bear
a superficial resemblance to those of the contemporaneous
Mediterranean literatures reveal differences in principle: rime
and alliteration in these literatures are not accentual and occur
between identical sounds. Celtic verse ornament reflects an
awareness of aural correspondences and a subtlety in their
poetic use quite beyond the ornament in Mediterranean literatures.
Old Irish verse ornament affiliates significantly, as regards
alliteration and rudimentary consonance, with early Teutonic
verse ornament; and, as regards various major devices, with
Old Welsh verse ornament. One can scarcely invoke Latin
influence for Celtic-Teutonic affiliations that antedate the Roman
empire; or for Irish-Welsh affiliations that could take us to
druidic congresses.

● The *Hisperica Famina* is not 'rimed prose', as Wilhelm Meyer
supposed, but rather a group of concoctions in artificial languages
developed from Latin and Irish by a technique of distortion
(augmentation, diminution, reversal, etc. of syllables and letters)
—probably in vain emulation of the druidic 'secret' language
(that is, the proto-Goidelic of the ogham inscriptions) and of
oghamic cyphers such as are preserved in the Book of Ballymote.[10]

● The *Epitomes of Publius Virgilius Maro* (vм) is evidently a satire
on the *Hisperica Famina* and on the rustic Latinity and false
metrical quantities of early versifiers who were attempting
to use Celtic verse ornament in Latin.[11] The satirist was too
successful; his work has been taken seriously as scholarship.

● Kuno Meyer's slight pamphlet on the flight of Gaulish scholars is sheer speculation, so far as verse ornament is concerned. One need not doubt the scholar's flight to doubt their influence in Ireland (especially if they fled to Wales).[12]

Gaulish literature was orally transmitted (as Caesar observed) despite Gaulish acquaintance with Greek and Roman letters. Irish and Welsh literature continued to be orally transmitted well into the Christian period. (Oral transmission of course protected the prerogatives of a learned caste or class.) The paucity of literary remains from Celtic paganism has encouraged an aberrant tendency to regard the pagan Celts, before romanization or christianization, as illiterate barbarians living in an intellectual vacuum, whose culture must necessarily have originated externally. Yet the oral transmission of knowledge is compatible with an advanced state of learning; take Socrates, for instance, or the immense grammatical lore of early Sanskrit. Pythagoras (sixth century BC) apparently communicated on learned matters with the Celts of his environs. For centuries, beginning before the conquest of Gaul, a long line of Gallo-Roman poets and rhetoricians graced the Latin language. Vergil was a Celt. Caesar's tutor was a Celt, as was Caesar's intimate adviser throughout the Gallic wars—the noble Aeduan, the druid Divitiacus.

The Gaulish curriculum for literary study took up to twenty years for completion, as Caesar noted. A comparable curriculum for Ireland is detailed in an early source.[13] Are we to suppose that the Celtic poets who pursued these curricula, which were more demanding than any known to Greece or Rome, had no knowledge of such obvious devices as alliteration, rime, consonance and assonance throughout the centuries before romanization? Or that, once the Celts encountered simple hymns in Latin, likely sung to popular tunes, or the 'rimed prose' of, say, St Augustine, they straight away derived a complex system of verse ornament, based on accent and on a scientific phonetics, from Latin rudiments that as yet knew neither a stress system nor phonetics? To ask the question is to answer it.

Obviously, Old Irish verse ornament is uniquely phonetic in basis and uniquely systematic in application (chapters 4 and 5). Late Latin 'rimed prose' discloses neither the basis nor the applications that distinguish Old Irish verse. In the Latin prose, what

rime there is, is sporadic and non-accentual, and involves a correspondence of identical letters rather than of phonetically classed
sounds. Consonance, which is basic to Old Irish verse, does not
occur as an ornament in Latin prose. Irish rime and consonance,
by virtue of their basis and system, are further removed than even
Irish alliteration from Late Latin 'rimed prose'. In this prose,
alliteration occurs between identical letters only; it is for the
eye more than for the ear; it is not related to accent, and accented
syllables freely intervene between alliterating letters. Quite
clearly, in the light of the rules and incidence set forth in chapters
4 and 5, Late Latin 'rimed prose' contributed nothing to Irish
verse ornament. Hence, naturally, the terms used for alliteration
and for rime and its variants in early Irish prosodic treatises do not
derive from Latin.

Part IV : Proliferation and Diffusion

10

Proliferation

Though the origin of the rhythms, forms and ornament of early Celtic verse has been ascribed to prehistoric substrata and Indo-European archetypes, and though these traits show a conservative integrity of style, nevertheless they proliferated with vigour epochally, in response to linguistic and cultural change.

When proto-Goidelic and Brythonic became Old Irish and Old Welsh, the emergent languages were characterized by the loss of inflectional suffixes, by the rise of initial inflection and by the consequent tendency of accent to fall on a root syllable that was—in Irish usually, and in Welsh often—an initial. This linguistic change predisposed Celtic verse towards the cultivation of accentual rime, towards a shortened verse line and towards a tightened accentual structure. (EPP, p. 708)

Inasmuch as proto-Goidelic remained a ritual and professional language for centuries after the rise of Old Irish and Old Welsh (comparable to the survival of Vedic during the rise of Sanskrit or to the survival of Hebrew or of Church Latin), the consequent necessity of grammatical studies (as in ancient India) doubtless occasioned the discovery of the passably scientific phonetics which became the basis of Old Irish rime, consonance and assonance.[1] A revision in the structure of the ogham alphabet, made before the Goidelic adoption of Roman letters, reflects this *new* phonetics. (The ogham alphabet, a cypher for a finger language, was used for memorials in proto-Goidelic, during the decline of Irish paganism.) (MSLI, pp. 1–36)

One looks, therefore, to the centuries after Caesar but before Patrick for the impetus toward a cultivation of such poetic forms and rhythms as were termed *bardic* in the early Irish metrical tracts, as distinguished from the older *alliterative accentual* verse of the *filid* and the archaic utilitarian verse of the law tracts. It is the

113

bardic verse that utilizes lyric stanzas and a system of verse ornament based on the *new* phonetics: the older heroic verse and the
legal verse utilize an alliterative phonetics of ruder level.

The differences in form and ornament between early Welsh
and Irish verse, although insufficient to obscure the evidence
of common origin, yet signify an extended period of independent
development. This independence could have been enforced on
Britain by the onset of its Roman conquest, by its christianization,
and by its Germanic invasions. A common Irish-Welsh literary
and prosodic development was possible so long as druidism united
the learned classes of Ireland and Wales; but British druidism
was apparently stultified by the Roman conquest and its aftermaths
—Christianity and the Germanic influx. It is significant that the
ogham memorials of Wales and Scotland occur only in the areas of
extensive Irish settlement.

We posit, then, a long period of evolution for the Old Irish and
Old Welsh poetries, anterior to their first documentation in the
sixth century AD, when a whole panoply of poetic forms begins
to be documented—a whole technique of structure and ornament
that for subtlety of effect and complexity of organization must
surely be accounted among the artistic wonders of the world.
It is certain that the foundations of the new phonetics were established in Ireland long before the date of the earliest available
Old Irish verse that reflects the new phonetics (that is, long before
the sixth century AD). It is not implausible that centuries should
have passed between the first application of the new phonetics
to verse and the first documentation, in the sixth century AD,
of the matured and highly complex system of verse structure
and ornament described here. Celtic poetic art could no more
have sprung into existence at a stroke, as it were, than could
the comparably complex and traditional Celtic art of design and
ornament in metal, in stone and on manuscript—an art that
developed organically from at least the La Tène and even the
Megalithic epochs and whose artifacts, being tangible, permit
of the direct verification of historic concepts; whereas the literary
evidence, having been preserved orally, permits of a reconstruction
only by proper analysis and the comparative method.

Irish metrical tracts of the ninth, tenth and eleventh centuries
provide evidence of the proliferation of stanzaic forms. These
tracts reveal, by their occasional conflicts in terminology, the

existence of traditions considerably older than the tracts; and by their extensive community of terms, the operation of a central tradition.

It has been determined, from a count of the varieties described in the metrical tracts and the varieties known from other sources, that at least 350 forms existed in Old Irish verse. (HLHI, p. 488) This number, though perhaps astonishing, is not unprecedented: 150 treatises in Sanskrit disclose 850 forms (EPP, pp. 394-95), and Icelandic variants of just the rímur have been attested as at least 2000. (EPP, p. 711) Only a few dozen formal species in each corpus of verse, however, appear with any frequency.

During the efflorescence of rhythms, forms and ornament which attended the once new epochs of Old Irish and Old Welsh, an indefinitely extensible number of variant forms became possible. One can readily credit the possibility of an indefinitely extensible proliferation of forms merely on considering the possible per-mutations and combinations of stanzaic pattern within the systems of forms that emerge at relatively primitive levels. We referred above (pp. 28-30) to the fourteen variants of the elemental triad, derivable by incremental repetition. When to this triad one adds the refrain of but a single line, the triadic quatrain that ensues can exist in four times the fourteen triadic variants, merely by placement of the refrain as first, second, third or fourth line. These fifty-six variants, with the fourteen original, total seventy. If the refrain should then consist of two lines added to the original fourteen triadic variants in each of four positions, an additional fifty-six variants ensue; or a total of 126. The contraction or expansion of the basic triad by one line would double the 126 possible variants, giving a total of 252.

If we now consider the possibility of variants at a slightly higher level of triadic utterance—the tripartite statement (pp. 31-32) rather than the triple iteration—the same arithmetic will apply. In addition, the possibility of formal modification in the duration of each line of the tripartite statement provides a vastly enlarged capability of formal variety. If to this triadic capability we add the capability of formal variation derivable from the primitive couplet, consisting of balanced statements appositional or antithetic as in the Hebrew psalms or the earlier Assyrian-Babylonian wisdom literature, a variety of form certainly adequate to primeval ex-pressive needs is seen to have been readily available to the early poet, provided that he had a modest ingenuity in the manipulation of binary and ternary statement.

At levels of poetic art where structure and ornament became sufficiently generalized to exist as patterns regardless of specific content—the levels completely achieved in Celtic verse by the time of its earliest documentation and manifestly for centuries before— the possibilities of formal variation within the limits of stanza are well-nigh incalculable, because of the manifold variants: kind of rhythm, number and length of verse line, incidence of caesura, structure of cadence or verse-end, variety and combination of ornament, placement of ornament, class of stanza, etc. Of the many thousand possible formal variants within the Celtic stanza of limited compass, the poets arrived at a relatively quite limited consensus in actual practice.

We must grant, of course, the loss of many variants through the vagaries of oral transmission and the sort of selectivity that monastic clerks would understandably exercise in regard to verse irreconcilably pagan in purport, and also because of changes in fashion and the transitional nature of much experiment.

Analogous forms of verse almost certainly had currency in both Wales and Ireland; yet the early literatures of these two closely affiliated countries preserve, in some cases, merely traces of forms in the one literature that survive copiously in the other. Thus, the triadic stanza and the epic-elegiac *laisse* survive richly in early Welsh, and slightly in early Irish; whereas the quatrain and the heroic verse of paired stresses, richly surviving in early Irish, are scantily evident in the earliest Welsh. Such circumstances probably reflect the selectivity of copyists who began to document Celtic verse only after centuries of relatively independent Welsh-Irish literary development, rather than the actualities of Welsh and Irish poetic form during the pre-documentary period, which was also the probable period of greatest formal variety and efflorescence, judging not only from the Vedic-Sanskrit analogue but especially from the rhythmic and ornamental variety of what Kuno Meyer, at the close of his career, termed 'die älteste irische Dichtung'.

Here, at the onset of documentation, appears a far greater variety of basic verse forms than characterizes later Celtic centuries: the epic-elegiac line of *Y Gododdin;* the richly incremental *laisses* of the early Welsh epic and elegy; the torrential processions of paired stresses in Old Irish panegyric, epic dialogue and lyric;

the triadic stanza of Llywarch Hen and Heledd; the rimeless stanzas that yet rime in last lines only; the freely accentual quatrains with highly regular riming verse-ends; the structurally regular yet rimeless quatrains of certain Old Irish genealogies; the Old Irish elegies attributed to Dallan Forgaill; the shamanistic satires, curses, prophecies, incantations and prayers—whence passed this richness, preserved to us in a mere sporadic scattering by who knows what fugitive devotees within the walls of monasteries happily not entirely Christian.

We have noted (pp. 7-16) how regulated variation in the modes of *word foot* and *word measure* rhythm occasion stanzaic patterns whose syllabic count becomes the signature of stereotypes recognizable centuries later in the surviving metrical tracts. The emergence of the Celtic verse foot ensured a still further regulation of rhythm in early stanzaic patterns. But as Celtic speech grew gradually uno-accentual over the centuries, the Celtic verse foot diminished in significance as an organizational element for the verse line; until (well into the Middle Irish period) the accentual requirement of the verse-end, operating reflexively within the by now traditional structural frame of multifarious stanzaic patterns, ensured a continuance of early rhythmic styles, subject to modification inevitably imposed by drift from an Old Irish speech that was frequently bi-accentual to a Middle Irish that was becoming preponderantly uno-accentual.[2] The drift in speech accent tended to produce verse rhythms comparable to those of dry speech, within a verse structure whose syllabic dimensions had derived from bi-accentual rhythms. Hence the Late Classical Irish verse line tends to be capable of scansion as reflecting an iambo-trochaic rhythm that still continues one unique aspect of the bi-accentual Celtic verse foot—its freedom of alternation between iambic and trochaic stresses.

Diffusion

The diffusion of Celtic verse form and ornament bears two aspects:
internal, among Celts; external, from Celts to others.

The Impact of Christianity

The triumph of Christianity in Ireland, by the late sixth century,
had temporarily upset the stability of Irish society, especially
as regards the position and prestige of the druids and the high
poets. The advent of a new learning, a new pantheon and a new
sacred language had the practical effect of lowering the values
attached to the old. The druid as diviner, the druid as supervisor
of rituals, the druid as purveyor of the knowledge that brings
power—in these relations, the druid began to pass away. In his
place arose the Christian, or rather the Irish, saint. The poet
schools continued, but with formidable competition from the
monastic schools. The bards, once mere entertainers of the people,
proved useful to the evangelizing saints for the writing of hymns
and sacred songs sung doubtless to melodies of the people. The
high poet, to whom the bard had once been subordinate, now found
the bard a rival. To survive, the high poets (*filid*) compromised:
bardic measures became an increasing part of the high poet's
practice.

Fortunately for Irish art, the Irish social structure supported
monastic Christianity, during the century and a half after
Patrick, and rejected the episcopal form of church organization,
based on Roman urbanism. (CEIS) In consequence, the saint
and the abbot came to enjoy the same privileged status as the high
poet, without entirely supplanting him.[3] In the arts of decoration
and design traditional techniques and motifs survived, and the
new Christian motifs blended with the pre-existing pagan motifs
and style. (HIEP) In poetry, the new subject matter and new
pantheon began to be enshrined in traditional verse—for the most
part, bardic verse—and monks began to document the pagan
sagas, under the inspiration of a Christianity already Celtic. By

the eighth century, Irish Christianity was assiduously cultivating what it doubtless took to be the best of both worlds—the literature and art of Celtic tradition, and the piety and learning of the Church. Further, Irish Christianity had become the possession of the great families—the monasteries their fiefs, the abbots their kinsmen. (CEIS)

Celtic verse forms, which had proliferated richly during the pre-documentary Old Irish and Old Welsh epochs, experienced a diminution in spectrum with the triumph of Christianization but also an accretion in subject matter and a change in spirit. Worthies of the Church became the subject of panegyric; and the poetic technique cultivated originally for the praise of heroes was applied, with utmost art, to the praise of the Virgin and the saints.

The change in spirit that permitted the writing down of traditional verse and saga signified the passing, to some extent, of the hierarchical gradations that, under traditional law, stratified the corps of poets, and the forms proper to their grades.[4] The most skilled poets increasingly devoted themselves to cultivation of the measures originally bardic, with the result that the measures of bardic verse became increasingly stereotyped. The niceties that distinguish their varieties, in the metrical tracts of the ninth, tenth and eleventh centuries, attest also to the complexity that best serves the professional. The existence of these tracts proves not only that the strictly oral tradition of the ancients was weakening, but that the bardic measures—which no doubt were originally easy and for the ordinary people—had now become the complex crafts of a new breed of high poet.

In Wales, the same distinction early existed in law and in fact between the high poet and the poet as entertainer. Because the Britons for centuries had been on the defensive, both culturally and militarily, the opportunity had not arisen to develop freely the niceties of legal distinction that prevailed in Ireland; yet the basic differences in class and function persisted in both Wales and Ireland—just as they had existed in pre-Caesarian Gaul.[5]

In Ireland, the musician had separate status from the poet; nevertheless, the bards sang the verses of the high poet when they travelled in his retinue. The practice in Wales was apparently less specialized. If it had been like the Irish practice in earlier centuries, it was no longer so by the time of Gruffydd ap Cynan's reconquest of Wales (circa 1135). One of Gruffydd's major tasks, on reestablishing Welsh power, was to distinguish poetry and music

E

as separate professions, in accordance with the practice in Ireland, where he had been reared (his mother was Irish). The *Institutes* of Gruffydd ap Cynan attest this accomplishment.[6]

Irish-Welsh Affiliations

The intimate relations of Wales and Ireland persisted until the Norman Conquest. These relations had involved pre-Christian settlements of Irish in Wales and of Welsh in Ireland, the Christianization of Ireland largely from Wales, and the exchange of literary and artistic elements such as story matter and design motifs.

The affiliations of Irish and Welsh poetic techniques reflect development from similar origins, but not extensive imitation. The influence of these techniques upon each other was perhaps less substantial than their influence on the technique of Latin verse in Ireland and Wales. The appearance of monorime in Cambro-Latin verse paragraph and stanza and the use of monorime in certain Latin poems in the Old Irish *Antiphonary of Bangor* (the monastery of Bangor was established by Welshmen) seem indication enough that Cambro-Latin verse drew on the technique of an existing Welsh verse no different in its end-rime from the monorime *laisse* of Aneirin or from his *debide* couplets:

> Gratum fecit Fintenanum
> Heredem almum inclitum,
> Illustravit Maclaisreum
> Kaput abbatum omnium,
> Lampade sacrae Seganum
> Magnum scripturae medicum
>   Quos convocavit Dominus
>   Coelorum regni sedibus   AB, II,   p. 33[7]

> finit opus in domino
> othei quiri altisimo
> meo patre commoneo
> scriptum simul ac magistro.   CA,   lxxiv

Riming couplets of course characterized Old Irish *debide* also. It seems likely, however, that the riming couplets and the four-line runs of monorime in such early Hiberno-Latin verse as the *Altus Prosator* of Colum Cille, whose Christianity derived from Wales, represent Hiberno-Latin imitation of Cambro-Latin verse, rather than of native Irish verse. The Columban verse does not observe the *debide* requirement that one of the verse-ends in each couplet should rime on the accent, nor does the Cambro-Latin monorime. The Columban and the Cambro-Latin couplets in fact rime non-accentually.[8]

Some decades later, *Munther Benchuir beata* combines monorime on a final letter with accentual end-rime. In this sort of rime, one inclines to see a response to both Welsh and Irish vernacular verse—the monorime Welsh, the accentual rime Irish. The apparent failure of poets using the Irish language to adopt the combination of accentual rime with monorime on a final letter or syllable is one more indication that the vernacular poets did not mimic the saints writing verses in Latin.

This is not to maintain that the Welsh and Irish techniques of vernacular verse remained completely independent. The extensive movement of Irish population into southwest and northwest Wales during the early Christian centuries occasioned the Welsh acquisition of much Irish story material. Although assimilated to Welsh literature and language, this material retains sufficient trace of its origins to permit its derivation from Ireland.

Did the prose tale with verse highlights come as a form to Wales from Ireland with the story material? And to Brittany from Wales, from Ireland, or from both? In the absence of documentation, any of this is possible. But it is at least equally possible that the form represents a common Celtic inheritance, with Indo-European antecedents: the same form appears in Sanskrit story.

The strong evidence adduced here for the indigenous development of Old Irish and Old Welsh verse, and for its germinal influence on Hiberno-Latin and Cambro-Latin verse, gives confidence that a Gaulish verse of comparable antecedents had a germinal influence on a Late Latin popular verse, both secular and religious, and consequently on the verse of the emerging Romance languages. Such Gaulish influence would also afford an explanation for the sporadic appearance of experiments in monorime or assonance, as in poems by Commodian in the third century and, later, St Augustine.

Gaulish Ausonius (c. 310 to c. 393 AD), an eminent poet in Latin yet also the scion of druids, has left a Latin poem in which the last word of each line is a monosyllable (as in the Old Irish verse measure *rannaigecht mor*) which is repeated as the first word of the next line (as in Old Irish *conachlonn*), and in which the last word of the poem repeats its first (as with the Old Irish rule for finishing a poem). (SESS, p. 32) Inasmuch as Ausonius testified to the continued use of the Gaulish language in his day, one inclines to see, in his Latin poem, a reminiscence of techniques employed in Gaulish verse as in Old Irish.

The practical certainty that the hymns of Ambrose were sung to tunes previously familiar to members of his congregation, and that the early Christian evangelizers composed hymns comparable in Ireland and elsewhere to the music of the people, makes it plausible to conclude that the sort of ornament termed 'Ambrosian' (Part II, pp. 70-73) reflects a popular usage in the Late Latin verse of Gaulish provenance. The tendency of this ornament toward end-assonance invites us to view the end-assonance of the earliest Old French and Old Spanish verse as a continuation of Gaulish and Celtiberian Late Latin verse.

Comparative analysis of Old Welsh and Old French verse establishes the probability that their common traits, particularly in the structure and ornament of the *laisse*, reflect indebtedness of Old French to Old Welsh in some respects, and independent development from a Common Celtic source in others. The Celtic provenance of the *laisse* is strongly indicated.

Celtic and Anglo-Saxon Affiliations

It is not least among the ironies of history that, while British Celt and Saxon joined in struggle to the death, Irish Celt and Angle joined in the peaceable quest for eternal life. Ireland, indebted primarily to Wales for the contours of its Christianity, brought the True Light in turn, through Iona, to the foes of Wales. Angles and Saxons soon flocked to Ireland for instruction even as their brothers assailed Wales to its devastation. Posterity owes this irony two epics: *Y Gododdin*—its composition, and *Beowulf*—its survival.

Hiberno-Saxon Christianity in Northumbria tended toward a symbiosis, as in Ireland, of pagan and Christian values. Where the Roman rite had temporarily prevailed in parts of England, the tendency was strong to extirpate native culture-elements and to establish a church whose organization was episcopal and urban.[9] Where the Roman rite held sway, no epic verse survived in

England, and scarcely any native literature. It was Irish Christian cultivation of the bard and the story-teller, expressed transcendently in the apotheosis of Colum Cille as poet-saint, that set a pattern for Northumbria and indeed for all areas where Irish Christianity prevailed.[10] Hence the Caedmonian lays, the Anglo-Saxon conversion of Biblical worthies to Celtic-Teutonic heroes, and the preservation by Northumbrian clerics of *Beowulf, Finnsburg, Wanderer* and *Widsith*. Hence indeed, as in Ireland, the use of indigenous dialects as languages of Christian learning, rather than their extirpation in favour of Church Latin.

The elements of decoration, being more abstract than the elements of linguistics, permit of readier cultural transference. The affiliation of Irish and Northumbrian arts is therefore notably manifest in design on metal and manuscript. In contrast, the highly developed literature and language of Northumbria persisted, substantially unaffected by the grammar and prosody of Old Irish. The poetry of Northumbria, whether of pagan or Christian background, owed to Irish Christianity not so much technique as the encouragement of cultivation and preservation. Even so, the *riming poem* (a West Saxon version of an eighth-century Northumbrian original) obviously reflects a style verified in early Celtic verse; and *Elene* has an extended passage in comparable rime.

In Anglian and Saxon Latin, more than in the vernacular, one notices the influence of Irish linguistics and prosody. Words from Hisperic Latin appear in the Latin of Aldhelm, as in that attributed to Colum Cille.[11] Anglo-Latin hymns survive, on the model of Hiberno-Latin hymns. (Their characteristics as an aspect of the diffusion of Celtic versecraft through Latin are discussed below on pages 138-141.)

A diffusion of Celtic versecraft from Wales to the adjoining Anglo-Saxon areas of Britain occurred after the stabilization of political relations. The Scandinavian invasions and especially the Norman conquest of England gave common cause to the submerged Welsh and Saxons. Alfred maintained amicable relations with the Welsh church, and drew steadily upon the assistance of Welsh and Irish scholars in his efforts to restore and revitalize the intellectual life of England, after his victories over the Danes. Following the Norman Conquest, the struggle for freedom in England shifted from a contest of Celt and Saxon to a contest uniting Celt and Saxon against the Norman overlord. At the same time, the centralization of power by the Norman government diminished, to a considerable degree, the vogue of semi-tribal conflict that had kept the Celts and Saxons in turmoil both among themselves and against each other.   The poetry of Middle English henceforth begins to exhibit Celtic traits, at both the popular and learned levels. *Sumer is icumen in* has Celtic stanzaic form.   It is the lyric (likely a translation, certainly an imperfect fit) to music of Celtic provenance (the *Reading Rota*).[12]   Layamon's *Brut* has obvious affiliations with Welsh literature.[13]   The verse termed *Skeltonic* is an English variant of a stanzaic form common to Welsh for centuries before its appearance in English.[14]   The poet of *Pearl* and of *Sir Gawain and the Green Knight* combines a creative use of Anglo-Saxon alliterative versecraft with stanzaic devices whose provenance is Celtic.[15]   Shakespeare makes bantering use of Skeltonics to satirize rustic versifiers.

Celtic and Norse-Icelandic Affiliations

The affiliation of Celtic versecraft with Germanic, though it extends to prehistoric times (pp. 86-90), becomes most substantial in the interrelations of Celtic and Scandinavian poetries.   The Viking settlements in Ireland and Wales were a bridge for the passage of Celtic culture-elements from the Western Isles to Norway and especially Iceland.

The Norse-Irish kingdom of Dublin facilitated cultural interchange.   The arts of design and decoration testify to an extensive borrowing of motifs and styles, primarily by the Norse, but also by the Irish.   In the arts of war both by land and sea, the Irish learned hard lessons from the Norse, which later assisted in defence against the Normans.   In poetry, the debt was repaid.

Icelandic verse combined the basic Germanic structure with Celtic ornament.   Although Welsh influence cannot be entirely discounted, the preponderance of derived elements is Irish. (TIRC)

It is possible that Skaldic verse had become stanzaic before the period of Celtic influence.   The traditional diction of such verse continues the style of Eddic diction and, indeed, typically exceeds it in complexity of kenning.   The ornament of Skaldic verse, as of Eddic, consists heavily of intralinear rime and consonance which, to some extent, could have developed indigenously.[16]

The typical line lengths of Skaldic verse relate to the Eddic verse line of paired stresses.   Whereas the Eddic line, like the

Anglo-Saxon, freely admits unstressed syllables, the Skaldic line regulates their incidence. This tightening and normalizing of the line achieves an end result comparable to the Old Irish line regulated by *word foot* or *word measure* rhythm; that is, the regulation of rhythm enforces uniformity in the syllable count of the verse line. But whereas the typical use of *word measure* in the second half of the Old Irish verse line tends to perpetuate the cadential structure of a seven-syllable verse line that echoes Indo-European archetypes, the paired stresses of the early Germanic verse line tend to create half-lines of equal syllabic length. Hence the Skaldic stanzas are typically lines of six syllables and of eight syllables. On this basis, the Skaldic verse line of even-numbered syllable count, with caesura at mid-line, would appear to proceed organically from the Eddic line of paired stresses—very likely in response to musical regulation. The frequently used early Celtic verse lines of typically odd-numbered syllable count—especially seven and nine—appear not to have influenced early Norse poetry.

The ornament of Icelandic poetry is distinctive for the frequency and systematic use of intralinear rime and consonance. The ornament termed *aðelhending* consists of full syllabic rime between two syllables within the verse line:

gram reki b*ond*af l*ond*um

The ornament termed *skothending* consists of intralinear correspondence between two syllables whose vowels differ, but whose post-vocalic consonants are identical:

Sva sk*yld*i goð gj*ald*a

In the stricter forms of *Drottkvaett* (Court Metre), *skothending* occurs in the first line of the couplet; *aðalhending*, in the second. Both ornaments engage the last stressed syllable of the verse line.

A comparison of intralinear rime and consonance among Icelandic (tenth century), Welsh (ninth century) and Irish (seventh century) poetries discloses important similarities.

The simplest species of consonance that involves a correspondence of more than a single consonant or consonant group is termed, in traditional Welsh prosody, *cynghanedd fraidd-gyfwrdd*:

Icelandic

  Sol varp *sunn*an *sinn*i mána   JAWS,   p. 8
  Lá *né lœt*i, *né lit*a goða   JAWS,   p. 8

Welsh

  Neur di*g*ereis a *g*araf   CLH,   p. 9, v. 4, 1. 3
  *b*erwyt *b*ryt *b*ra*t*   CLH,   p. 26, v. 23, 1. 3
  *G*oreu *g*wr *G*aranmael   CLH,   p. 45, v. 92, 1. 3

Irish

  sech *dr*u*ng*u *d*e*mn*e   STP II,   p. 325
  ro*r*óina *r*eu*nn*   STP II,   p. 325
  di*u*dercc *nd*ēr   MMH,   p. 27

Nida *d*īr *d*ermait	*d*āla cach *r*īg *r*ōm*d*ai,
*r*eimse *r*īg Temro	*t*ūatha for *slicht slōgd*ai.
Sōer *c*a*thm*īl *cōem*f*ata	*M*ōen *L*a*b*raid *Long*sech,
leo *n*ī*th*ach, *nathch*obir,	*cathch*obir com*sech*.
*Cathm*il *A*ilill *fi*i āga	fri *crīcha Crothom*uin,
*croth*ais *A*bra*tch*āin	air*be* ī*ath* n*Eth*omuin. MAID I, pp. 16–17

Several varieties of consonance possess structural as well as
ornamental significance, since they tend to underline or create
rhythmic divisions. In the variety termed *cynghanedd groes* in
traditional Welsh prosody, the verse line tends to fall into two
parts and the consonance is so placed as to emphasize this division:

Icelandic

  Eit*t* es *m*ál þa*ts m*æla   JAWS,   p. 8

Welsh

  *T*ei*th* odef, *tuth* hebawc   CLH,   p. 24, v. 10, 1. 22
  *M*eu *g*erit; *m*i a'e *g*oruc   CLH,   p. 31, v. 9, 1. 3
  *Ott*i*d* eiry; *t*ohi*d* istrad   CLH,   p. 27, v. 5, 1. 1
  *N*i*d u*i*d* yscol*eic; n*i*d v*i*d* e *leic*, vnben   CLH,   p. 31, v. 11, 1. 1

Irish

  lam *n*óib di *L*aig*n*i*b*   STP II,   p. 326
  *L*e*thch*olbe *flath*o   STP II,   p. 326
  ar *cuirp* hi *cilicc*   STP II,   p. 326
  *D*ī*a m*ār m'anacul *d*e *m*uir theintidiu   MMH,   p. 27

The *Heimskringla* of Snorri Sturluson contains over one hundred examples of a form of consonance—termed in Welsh prosody *cynghanedd draws*—in which the verse line tends to fall into three parts as a result of the placement of the ornament:

Icelandic

> *G*um*n*a vinr at *g*am*n*i JAWS, p. 8
> *F*old*d*ar rauð ok *f*eld*d*i JAWS, p. 8
> *Gri*þum vér i *grei*þar JAWS, p. 8
> *S*en*d*ir fell á *s*an*d*i JAWS, p. 8

Welsh

> Bu*teir* ennwir gynn*deir*yawc CLH, p. 34, v. 8, l. 2
> *K*yn*d*ylan Wynn uab *K*yn*d*rwyn CLH, p. 34, v. 13, l. 1
> *bu* trydar ea aerure *bu* tan
> *bu* cut e waewawr *bu* *h*uan CA, p. 11, 11. 279-280
> *K*y*wyr*ein ketwyr *ky*w*r*en*h*in CA, p. 26, l. 656
> *n*y *ch*et*w*eist *n*ac ei*th*af *n*a *ch*ynnor (*n-ch-t*:*n-c-th*:*n-ch*)
> CA, p. 25, l. 636
> *r*ac *g*od*d*uryf y aessau*r* *g*od*d*echet (*r-cg-d*:*r-g-d*) CA, p. 48, l. 1223

Irish

> *Lab*raid lūam na *lergg*e
> *fagl*aid fri fūam *fairgg*e MAID I, p. 6, fn. 1

A distinctive kind of rime involves syllables other than the final. In Icelandic and Irish usage, this rime typically involves accented syllables. In early Welsh usage, a coincidence of accent and rime is not an essential trait.

Icelandic

> jalks br*ík*tǫpuð gl*ík*an JAWS, p. 7

Welsh

> am dry*n*ni *dryl*aw *dryl*enn CA, p. 19, l. 459
> ar gynt a gw*ydyl* a phr*yd*en CA, p. 20, l. 492
> na bei *kynh*awal *kynh*eilweing CA, p. 20, l. 507
> nyt *emd*a daear nyt *emd*uc mam; CA, p. 22, l. 555
> o gyvle *angh*eu o *angh*ar dut CA, p. 22, l. 559

Irish

  ind *rí*gin *rí*gde STP II, p. 326

  *nim*e *nim*reilge MMH, p. 27

  *fí*ri*ēn fí*rocus MMH, p. 27

  Aed oll fri *an*dud n*an*e STP II, p. 295

  Ropo *chē*tach *cē*tbliadnach MMH, p. 20

  A *Amor*gein *ānmol*taig MMH, p. 21

Another kind of rime involves the final syllable of one word and the penultimate of another:

Icelandic

  Allsv*angr* g*o*tur l*angar* JAWS, p. 7

  Fylkis *orð*, at m*orð*i JAWS, p. 7

Welsh

  Neut diann*erch* vy *erch*wyn CLH, p. 9, v. 5, 1. 3

  Bydaut dol*ur* pan b*ur*er CLH, p. 26, v. 24, 1. 2

  K*int*eic gu*int*; creilum coed CLH, p. 28, v. 13, 1. 1

  Y ar *can kan*lin Owein CLH, p. 28, v. 16, 1. 3

Irish

  donfé don bithflaith STP II, p. 325

  *cath*u *cach* -thedme STP II, p. 325

  *Ind fí*róg *in*main STP II, 326

  *lái*chd*u ó*caib, *ú*allch*u mú*rib MPIM, p. 2

Intralinear rime and consonance were interlaced and concentrically placed, thus constituting ornament analogous to that which appears in Celtic metal work and illumination:

Icelandic

  Naðr fr*ánn* neðan fra niðafjöllum (*n-ð-:fr-n-ð-:fr-n-ð-*)

                                                  JAWS, p. 8

Welsh

  Deil cwyd*it*; divr*yt* divro (*d-vr-:d-vr-*) CLH, p. 24, v. 13, 1. 2

  Crei vym br*yt*; cleu*yt* a'm cur (*cr-m-:m-c-r*)

                                            CLH, p. 25, v. 21, 1. 3

Coc vreue*r* yn Abe*r* Cuawc (*c-c-* :*c-c-*) CLH, p. 24, v. 10, l. 3

Ny chel gru*d* kystu*d* callon (*n-ch-l-* :*c-ll-n*) CLH, p. 26, v. 28, l. 3

Gwyr a gryssyassa*nt* bua*nt* gytneit (*g-r* :*gr*/*nt* :*n-t*)

hoedyl vyrryo*n* medwo*n* uch med hidleit. (*h-d, m-d* :*m-d, h-d*)

gosgord vynyda*wc* enwa*wc* en reit. (*rd-en* :*en-r-t*)

gwerth eu gwle*d* o ve*d* vu eu heneit. (*g* :*g*/*v* :*v*)

CA, p. 14, ll. 353–356

Irish

in gré*n* ti*nd* tóidlech (*t-nd* :*t-dl-*) STP II, p. 325

in*d* rígi*n* rígde (*rig* :*rig*)—rhyme STP II, p. 325

Sōer cathmīl cōemḟata   Mō*en* Labraid Lońgsech (*c-thm-* :*c-mf-*)

(*l-br* :*l-ng*)

leo nī*thach*, na*thchobir, cathchobir* comsech (*n-th-ch* :*n-thch-*) (*ch-b* :*c-m*)

MAID I, pp. 16–17

Dīa mār m'anacul de muir theinti*diu, diudercc ndēr* (*d-m-r* :*d-m-r*)

MMH, p. 27

It has been theorized that the Icelandic use of intralinear rime and consonance was derived from Welsh sources (JAWS). Though these kinds of ornament were employed in Welsh poetry before the development of an Icelandic literature, and though there were contacts between Wales and Iceland during the formative period of this literature, the thoery of Welsh derivation is nevertheless untenable, for two reasons: (1) Irish poetry that antedates the oldest surviving poetry in Welsh by two or three centuries employs all the kinds of intralinear rime and consonance common to the early poetry of both Wales and Iceland, and (2) Irish contacts with Iceland were more numerous, intimate and continuous than those of any other people save the Scandinavian.

The Irish visited and lived in Iceland before the Norse and possibly led the Norse there. The Norse settlers found a group of Irish monks in Iceland. Many of the Norse settlers had lived in Celtic territory, and many of the most influential, with the largest retinues of Celts, came from the 'Western Isles'. Of these Celts the Irish were by far the most numerous. The proportion of Celtic blood in the original Icelandic population has been estimated to have been as high as fifty percent, with thirty percent a conservative figure. Iceland maintained political and cultural relations with the Norse-Irish kingdom of Dublin. Irish poets visited

Iceland and Icelandic poets visited Ireland. Various of the Icelandic poets were partly or chiefly of Irish blood. Irish mythological and literary material was utilized in Icelandic literature. Words of Irish origin occur in the Icelandic vocabulary. A number of Icelandic place names are of Irish origin or associations.[17]

All the historical evidence of the Irish role in Icelandic culture leads to the presumption that the Icelandic use of intralinear rime and consonance derives principally from Irish sources; and yet to maintain this view would be to oversimplify.

First, the possibility of Welsh influence cannot be entirely excluded, particularly considering that *cynghanedd draws*, in which the verse line tends to fall into three parts as a result of the placement of the consonance, is common in both Icelandic and Welsh poetry, but uncommon in surviving Irish; and that the interlacement and concentric placement of intralinear rime and consonance which occur (uncommonly) in early Icelandic poetry are perhaps more like the Welsh methods of interlacing these ornaments than the Irish. Nevertheless, this possibly greater similarity between Icelandic and Welsh usage may in both instances merely reflect the greater similarity between Icelandic and Welsh verse structure— a phenomenon not attributable to Welsh influence—or, just possibly, in the case of *cynghanedd draws*, the increased Welsh use of this ornament from the twelfth century on may reflect Icelandic influence exercised by the Norse and Irish poets who attended Gruffydd ap Cynan in his successful conquest of Wales from Dublin, and by the Welsh imitators of these poets.

Second, Irish influence on Icelandic verse was not such as to result in the adoption of the Irish system of phonetic classification as the basis of Icelandic rime and consonance. On the contrary, though there may be traces of the operation of the Irish system, the traditional Germanic alliterative phonetics continued to prevail.

Third, although the remarkable development of verse ornament in Skaldic poetry is probably attributable to a Celtic and chiefly an Irish impetus, certain kinds of intralinear rime and consonance occurred sporadically in early Germanic verse of indigenous inspiration:

> *bēn* zi *bēna, bluot* zi *bluoda*   HDV I,   p. 103
> *sp*enis mih mit dīnēm *w*ortun,
>   wili mih d*ï*nu *sp*eru *w*erpan   HDV I,   p. 103
> thū biguolen Si*n*thgunt, Su*nn*a, era *s*wister   HDV I,   p. 102

It would be unscientific to assume that the sporadic appearance
of similar ornament in the earliest Icelandic verse is the result
of Celtic influence, since the only assumption necessary to account
for such appearance is that Germanic traditions had continued to
prevail.

Evidently we must distinguish between Icelandic verse ornament
derived from the Celts and Icelandic verse ornament whose potentialities were brought to full realization as a result of Celtic influence.
Ornament of the first description appears to have included systematic end-rime, intralinear rime involving unaccented final syllables,
and interlaced and concentrically placed combinations of rime and
consonance:

Naðr fr*ann* ne*ð*an fra Niðafjöllum   (*n-ð-:fr-n-ð-:fr-n-ð-*)   JAWS,   p. 8

Ornament of the second description includes consonance and rime
of accented sound complexes (syllables etc.)   It is ornament of
this second description that is present in early Germanic verse:

Sol varp sunnan, sinni mána

thū biguolen Sinthgunt, Sunna, era swister

jalks bríktǫpuð glíkan

bēn zi bēna, bluot zi bluoda

Because of the parallels between early Germanic and early Icelandic
verse ornament, it seems clear that Celtic influence is not responsible
for the appearance of all the varieties of ornament, except alliteration, that occurred in Icelandic verse, but rather that the Celts
introduced some types of ornament and helped toward a fuller
realization of the potentialities of others.   Significantly, in this
connection, the development of a more intricate verse ornament
in Icelandic did not involve the immediate overthrow of the structure
of the older Eddic poetry; rather, Eddic poetry survived unaltered
in its basic accentual structure.   So far as Celtic inspiration enriched
the ornament of Eddic poetry, this poetry was not denaturalized,
but instead was brought to a fuller expression of the potentialities
implicit in its structure.   Celtic influence brought to Icelandic
verse not a sudden revolution but a realization of the possibilities
of Germanic verse.

To sum up:

Early Irish, Welsh and Icelandic poetries display in common a number of kinds of intralinear rime and consonance.

The theory of an exclusively Welsh source of Icelandic intralinear rime and consonance is untenable, since Irish influence was far stronger in Iceland than Welsh.

Celtic influence, largely Irish but surely also Welsh, led to a richer development of the ornament of Eddic poetry, led to a remarkable elaboration of ornament (and form) in Skaldic poetry, and led to the Icelandic use of kinds of intralinear rime and consonance not previously characteristic of Germanic poetry.

Varieties of intralinear rime and consonance common to early Celtic and Germanic poetry were organic consequences of the principle of Celtic-Germanic alliteration, and may well have been employed in both Celtic and Germanic poetry, in at least sporadic form, during the period of early Celtic-Germanic intimacy on the continent (Part II, pp. 86-90).

Old Welsh and Old French Affiliations

Y Gododdin and *Marwnad Cynddylan* offer numerous parallels in device to the Old French epics *La Chanson de Roland* and *Voyage de Charlemagne à Jérusalem et à Constantinople*. The Welsh poems are linguistically of the ninth century, though *Y Gododdin* is some centuries older in its core of historical substance and perhaps in some of its lines. The Old French epics mentioned date from the late eleventh or early twelfth century in their present form and are among the oldest surviving in French. They probably existed in earlier forms now lost. The significant parallels in device are as follows:

1. The poems are composed throughout in a series of strophes, and these are irregular in length.

2. The typical strophe is one in which all the verse lines are linked to one another by an identity or a close similarity in the sound of their final accented vowel (Old French) or final syllable (Old Welsh). That is, the Old French strophes—terminal *laisses*—are characterized by end-assonance; the Old Welsh, by end-rime.

3. The end of the strophe is usually strongly marked by the final clause or sentence, which is usually independent in syntax and summary, sententious or climactic in content.

4. Repetition of the end-rime or end-assonance is avoided in successive strophes.

5. There is usually a strophe for each distinct division of the substance: nearly always, the strophe forms a well-defined unit.

6. Occasionally in the Old French epics and frequently in the Old Welsh elegies, the substance of a strophe will be repeated in two or more successive strophes, in such a manner as to display various facets or aspects of the substance, either by the introduction of details previously undeveloped or by their development in another manner or from another point of view.

7. Successive strophes—and even separated strophes—sometimes display a close correspondence in the wording of their opening lines. This correspondence usually involves partial repetition and occasionally complete repetition.

8. The same sort of correspondence occurs between the closing lines of such strophes.

9. Strophes sometimes display a close correspondence of lines, phrases (sometimes stylized) or words, under circumstances other than those indicated in (7) and (8), above; for example, by repetition of elements interior to separated strophes, or in the last line of one strophe and the first line of the next.

10. Alliteration occurs very frequently as an ornament within the verse line and often as a link between successive verse lines.

11. Alliterating pairs of proper names (personages and places) occur in a characteristic manner. Sometimes, in the Welsh verse, more than two names will be involved in this alliteration.

The parallels presented above, though most frequent in *Roland* and *Voyage de Charlemagne*, are by no means confined to them. Rather, the *laisse* occurs in *Aucassin et Nicolette;* repetition of the opening lines of *laisses*, in *Aliscans* and other *gestes;* repetition involving groups of consecutive lines, in *Chançun de Williame;* repetition involving the opening lines of stanzas in the *Vie de Saint Léger;* repetition involving the closing lines of stanzas, in the refrains of romances and *pastourelles*. All eleven of the parallels presented above occur richly within the nine surviving strophes of *Marwnad Cynddylan* and, with varying frequency, in ninth-century Welsh poems attributed to Llywarch Hen.[18]

In the light of the parallels in poetic device between Old French and Old Welsh verse as presented above, it seems more than ever proper to maintain that the *laisse* 'was probably lyric in origin and early use.'[19] But did the technique of the Old French epic *laisse* develop from a lyric technique native to French, or was it derived from non-French sources? And was the origin and development of those traits indigenous, whereby the Old Welsh strophes appear to anticipate the Old French epic *laisse*?

Since the Welsh verse used for exemplifying the parallels in poetic device presented above is considerably older than any surviving Old French verse employing similar devices, and since the Celtic Church and the Celts in Brittany were active intermediaries for the passage of insular Celtic cultural elements to the continent, it would seem plausible to assume that the Old French usage of the *laisse* was modelled on Welsh lyric technique communicated through Brittany, were it not for the following differences in poetic device between the Old French *laisse* and its Old Welsh analogue:

> In the Old French epic, the verse lines of the *laisse* are linked by continuous assonance of their final accented vowel. In the Old Welsh elegies cited above, the verse lines of the strophe analogous to the *laisse* are linked by continuous rime of their end syllables. Indeed, assonance is scarcely employed as an end link in any surviving early Welsh verse.

> A far more intricate system of verse ornament is employed in the Old Welsh elegies than in the Old French poems. Various kinds of internal rime and consonance, and rich alliteration— all more or less systematically placed—characterize the Old Welsh strophes. The internal rime, the consonance and the systematic placement of ornament internal to the verse line cannot be verified as Old French usage.

> Caesura is definite and regular in the Old French epic *laisse;* sporadic and irregular, in the Old Welsh strophes analogous to the *laisse*.

The Welsh dwelt in Gaul before invading Britain. Their language developed from a form of Gaulish, and is closely related to what seem to be the major early Gaulish dialects. Equally many of the same Celtic peoples may have remained in Gaul as entered Britain. It is known that the Celts of Britain and Gaul maintained cultural and, probably, also political relations, until the Roman conquest. Celtic culture persisted in Gaul despite the Roman conquest, for both the Gaulish language and the institution of druidism were alive in Armorican Gaul (and apparently in other parts also) until at least the fifth century; and in this century the Welsh began to enter Brittany (Armorica) in large numbers. Since at least one element of traditional Celtic verse technique—alliteration—had become established in substantially its traditional form long before the Celts had crossed from the continent to Britain and Ireland, the more reason is there for supposing that traits of verse technique not only common to Welsh and Old French verse but uncommon in other west-European verse surviving from before the twelfth century did actually develop, perhaps to a large degree independently, from a Common Celtic source.

The geographical distribution of poetry exhibiting a verse form identical with, or similar to, the *laisse* includes France, Wales, Ireland, Italy, Spain and North Africa. It is obvious to regard France as a centre of influence in relation to the other lands named, purely on geographical grounds. On historical grounds, however, the case is at first glance less clear. The oldest evidence is North African: Commodian in the third century and Augustine in the fourth produced Latin poems that consist in long verse paragraphs, regular in rhythm, and knit by continuous mono-assonance and (sometimes) monorime. The *Antiphonary of Bangor*, a late seventh-century Irish manuscript, contains similar Latin poems. The Welsh epic, *Y Gododdin*, dates from the ninth century and possibly, in some of its substance at any rate, from the sixth century. An Italian manuscript preserves a Latin poem of the tenth century that has the same characteristics as the poems by Commodian and Augustine. The French material, by far the most extensive, is also the most recent of all save the Spanish.

It is evident that, regarding the *laisse*, one cannot base either geography or history on chronology, else one would be travelling from North Africa to Ireland through monastic channels, then in sequence to the bards of Wales, the monks of Italy and the minstrels of France. It is extremely unlikely that the *laisse* should travel so roundabout a route from Africa through Europe, in and out of monastic channels, enjoying a continued existence in only the secular and vernacular verse of Wales, France and Celtiberian Spain. It is not plausible to assume that the practice of the *laisse* reached France eight centuries after Commodian, following a circuit of western Europe, especially since there were close relations between Gaul and North Africa in the time of Commodian.

The Welsh use of the *laisse* is attended by more elaborate verse ornament than the non-Welsh use. The Welsh line-ends disclose full rime, not merely assonance as in France and Spain. The appearance of monorime in Bangor verse could reflect the strong Welsh influence on early Irish religious life. The Latin specimen in an Italian manuscript could reflect the influence of Irish monastics from Bangor. The Old French *laisse* could be an echo of Welsh practice, since Brittany was a bridgehead and a colony for Welshmen from the time of the invasion of Britain by the Angles and Saxons, But how account for Commodian's and Augustine's use of mono-rime ?

Both these writers spent some time in Gaul. In their day, Gaulish dialects were still spoken. Presumably, the character of Gaulish verse is reflected to some degree in the first Old French popular verse. And this popular verse perhaps remained fairly static in form and style until it was taken up by sophisticated poets. Further, this hypothetical Gaulish verse presumably influenced the character of the popular Latin verse practiced in Gaul. If the *laisse* is assumed to be a survival from Gaulish verse, it is easy to account not only for the appearance of mono-rime in poems by Commodian and Augustine, but also for the use of the *laisse* as the favourite verse form of the Old French epic.

Did the *laisse* travel, then, from Gaul to Britain ? Undoubtedly, when the Welsh themselves travelled from Gaul to Britain. Most of the known Gaulish dialects are closely related to Welsh in linguistic phenomena. When the 'Welsh' were 'Gauls', they must have shared a community of poetic technique with Gauls who remained on the continent. The *laisse* subsequently developed independently in Britain and Gaul. In Britain, it either preserved or acquired the ornament of full rime—if acquired, possibly under Irish influence. In Gaul, it survived the extinction of Gaulish in the fifth century or after, and lived on in the popular verse of Gallo-Latin and finally Old French.

Was monorime employed in this hypothetical Gallo-Latin verse ? We presume that Commodian and Augustine, in using the *laisse*, imitated Gallo-Latin popular religious verse. Later, Irish monks employed the *laisse*, very likely under the influence of Welsh monks who had presumably adapted the *laisse* to Cambro-Latin. And the Irish monks of Bangor, carrying their manuscripts to Bobbio, Monte Cassino and other Hiberno-Italic monasteries, provided models of the *laisse* for imitation in Latin.

Our hypothesis of the historical affiliations of the *laisse* is necessarily skeletal. But it coheres both internally and, more important, in relation to what is known of west European culture during the period involved. Further, the hypothesis is corroborated by the existence in Celtic lands, and in lands influenced by Celtic culture, of poems that terminate in each line with the letter *a*. The poem *Benchuir bona regula*, from the *Antiphonary of Bangor*, combines patterned accentual end-rime with this final *a* in each line. Other hymns of Irish provenance or style employ the *a* ending. Early French Sequences often end on the letter *a* in each line. An early Anglo-Latin poem has the same sort of ending, and so does an Old Irish quatrain quoted in *Cormac's Glossary*.

It has been conjectured that the *a* ending in the French Sequences was intended to echo the world *alleluia*. This conjecture would scarcely apply to the Old Irish quatrain, which appears to be of pagan background. The significant fact is the continuous ending of lines on a single letter throughout the verse paragraph. It is this that qualifies the poems just cited as further evidence of the Celtic provenance of the *laisse*; for the Sequence appears to have developed in its European form under the aegis of the Celtic rite,[20] and the Hiberno-Latin hymns were also a product of this rite.

Some may incline to a belief that the Celtic rite is the effective source of the *laisse*. The Celtic Church incorporated eastern and African elements. Augustine's hymn may have given birth to a poetic form, among Celtic churches, and the *Alleluia* echo on *a* may have firmly established it. Secular poets in Wales and France may then have taken up a rudimentary form of the *laisse* from the clerics and given it an artistic development.

Certain objections arise as to the theory of a Celtic rite rather than a Celtic race as the efficient cause of the *laisse*. First, no full-fledged *laisse* has survived from the Celtic rite of either Wales or France; yet it is in the secular poetry of these lands that the *laisse* reached fullest development. Second, specimens of the *laisse* in Welsh, though centuries earlier than French specimens, are nevertheless much more ornate and stylized; but if the Celtic rite was the source of the *laisse*, we should expect that its earlier imitations in the vernacular (as in Welsh) would be more rudimentary in verse technique than its later imitations (as in French). Third, the *laisse* appears in secular poetry only in Wales and France, lands of the p-Celts; and not in Ireland, a land of the q-Celts; yet the Celtic rite prevailed for centuries in all three lands.

These considerations, together with the relative slightness of the *a*-ending device as a specimen of the *laisse* technique, strongly suggest that the Celtic rite, so far as it cultivated anything like the *laisse*, merely reflected a popular verse form, just as the Hiberno-Latin hymns reflect, imperfectly for the most part, the technique of Old Irish bardic or popular verse. The Celtic rite, however, was probably the medium through which the *laisse* became known to North African and Irish clerics, just as the technique of Hiberno-Latin verse passed in a measure through the Celtic rite to England and the continent from Ireland.

In conclusion, the evidence examined supports the hypothesis that the *laisse* took its basic form among the p-Celts, Gaulish and Welsh; that it developed independently following the migration of the Welsh to Britain; that it was reflected in the Latin verse of the Celtic rite in France and Britain; that it became known to clerics in Africa and Ireland through such Latin verse; and that it passed from Irish to Italian monasteries.

Non-Celtic Latin Derivations

Irish poetry travelled throughout western Europe in the track of those Irish missionaries who left their homeland in a constant stream, in order to spread the faith among the still heathen Germanic peoples that had overrun most of the west, and to restore the faith wherever it had decayed, even beyond the Alps.

At first, the Irish laboured to convert the Picts of Scotland and the Germanic peoples that held most of England. At the same time, Ireland became an asylum for Britons who sought a pious or an intellectual life no longer possible on their home soil because of the ravages of the Anglo-Saxons. As evidence of the amicable relations between Ireland and Wales in the early Middle Ages, it may be worth noticing here that pieces in the *Liber Hymnorum* are attributed to Gildas and to the Welsh bishop Sanctan. As a result of the Irish mission to Anglo-Saxon Britain, a number of Anglo-Saxons wrote in what was obviously an attempt at the Irish style. The Irish influence may be traced in both the rhythm and the sound-harmony of Anglo-Saxon poets.

Aldhelm, born about 650 AD, began his studies at Malmesbury under the Irish teacher Maeldubh, and to the end of his life he professed a great admiration for Irish education. Aldhelm's verse does not show him to have been learned in Irish prosodic technique. Both his rime and his rhythm are anticipated by the *Altus* of Colum Cille, though his fondness for alliteration was hardly inspired by Colum Cille. It was not the lay but the monastic education of Ireland that Aldhelm knew. The nature of his indebtedness to Irish verse suggests that his teacher knew little or taught little of the technique of Irish verse in the vernacular, or in Latin, for that matter. The grotesque alliteration that appears in Aldhelm's prose suggest a possible indebtedness to Virgilius Maro, or to influences of the sort that Maro ridiculed. In fact, Aldhelm quotes Maro. (MSLI) Probably Aldhelm learned to take Maro seriously from the very type satirized by the grammarian. Aldhelm's fondness for Hisperic Latin hints that his Irish teachers belonged to the class of monastics that aped the druids and the *filid*, while lacking the knowledge to make the pretence convincing. It is striking that Aldhelm employs a kind of rime identical with that of the Irish Latin poems ascribed to St Colum Cille. This kind of rime comes closest of all Irish Latin rime to being an accurate echo of the form found in the unregulated bardic measures of the *Táin* (p. 25 above). The following quatrain is typical of Aldhelm use of rime:

> Christus passus patibulo
> atque leti latibulo
> virginem virgo virgini
> commendabat tutamini. RSLP I, p. 172

Notice the alliteration, Irish style, in each line. As in the Latin poems ascribed to St Colum Cille, the verse unit of eight syllables is employed.

Aldhelm appears to have set the style for a number of efforts by later English poets. For example, an unknown pupil of his writes as follows:

> elementa inormia atque facta informia
> quassantur sub aetherea convexi caeli camera,
> dum tremet mundi machina sub ventorum monarchia
>
> RCLP,   p. 145

Another pupil, Aethelwald, later a king of Mercia, writes as follows:

> ... spissam ceu aranea telam texit muscarea;
> tumque lana, latratibus fusi valde volantibus
> filatim quae revolvitur, veluti setis torquitur.
>
> RSLP, I,   p. 173

And, again, in another poem:

> manus, manus mirabiles, multum pedes placabiles,
> tibiae cursu teretes tam fortes, ut sonipedes
> saepe sequantur cursibus salientes praepetibus ...
>
> RSLP, I,   p. 173

The missionary Wynfrith, martyred in Frisia in 755 AD, wrote:

> vale, frater, florentibus
> iuventutis cum viribus,
> ut floreas cum domino
> in sempiterno solio,
> qua martyres in cuneo
> regem canunt aethereo,
> prophetae apostolicis
> consonabunt et laudibus,
> qua rex regum perpetuo
> cives ditat in saeculo.   RCLP,   p. 150

The rhythmic relation of these Anglo-Saxon poems to their Irish models becomes clear on comparison:

Christus passus patibulo   atque leti latibulo
Virginem virgo virgini   commendabat tutamini.

Altus prosator vetustus   dierem et ingenitus
Erat absque origine   primordii et crepidine.

An hypothesis of the Irish source of European patterned accentual
end-rime may be verified by reference to the presence of Irish Latin
poems with this kind of rime in manuscripts associated with various
European centres of learning and written at a date anterior to,
or else approximately contemporaneous with, the first appearance
of poems with patterned accentual end-rime composed by continental poets associated with these centres. For example, the
following poem, generally considered Irish, appears in the ninth-
century *Book of Prayers* of Aethelwald:

> Sancte sator, suffragator,
> Legum lator, largus dator,
> Iure pollens, es qui potens,
> Nunc in aethra, firma petra;
>
> A quo creta cuncta freta,
> Quae aplustra ferunt, flustra,
> Quando celox currit velox;
> Cuius numen crevit lumen,
> Simul solum, supra polum. . .[21]

Anglo-Saxon poets have left nothing from the ninth century, or
the tenth either, to match the rich dissyllabic accentual rime of
this poem to God. The frequent alliteration and the skillful manage-
ment of both alliteration and rime within the limiting compass of a
four-syllable verse unit distinguish the poem, and support the
belief in its Irish authorship.

It will be remembered that two poems from the *Antiphonary
of Bangor* end in every line on the letter *a*. This device crops up
in Italy, in the late ninth or early tenth century. A scholar of
Modena composed a poem to the defenders of that city, then in
danger from the Magyars, and ended all thirty-six lines of his poem
with the letter *a*. Another Italian poem, of the early tenth century,
consisting of nineteen quatrains, closes in every line of its last
eighteen quatrains on the letter *a*.[22] This poem is included in a
collection made up by Eugenius Vulgarius, who had been confined
for a while to Monte Cassino. Though there is no proof that the
authors of these Italian compositions ever saw the *Antiphonary of
Bangor*, their use of the *a* ending may bear some relation to the
fact that the *Antiphonary* left Bangor, soon after its last entry had
been made, for Bobbio, which was founded by monks of Bangor under
St Columbanus.

The *a* ending turns up in both England and France. All the lines, or many of the lines, in most of the Proses in the Anglo-Saxon *Tropary of Ethelred* close on the letter *a*. It is a characteristic of the oldest Sequences of France, currently considered the original source of the Sequence, that all the verses end either on the letter *a* or on an assonance on *a*, seemingly in order to echo the final *a* of the word *alleluia*, with which these Old French Sequences typically began. This ending on *a* in the Old French Sequences reflects, furthermore, the original form of the Jubilus— the root of the Sequence form—in which the final *a* of the *Alleluia* was prolonged to the accompaniment of a lengthy melody. Since current scholarship traces the Sequence form to the eighth century, it may be that the source of the Saxon *a* ending is French. But how is the *a* ending in Irish Latin poems of the late seventh century to be accounted for? And does the *a* ending in the Irish poems justify the suspicion that there may be an Irish source for the oldest form of Sequence known to France?

The degree to which Irish Latin poetry must have exercised an influence on the continent would never be suspected from a bare cataloguing of the continental manuscripts containing Irish Latin verse, relatively plentiful and satisfactorily early as these are. Irish missionaries and men of learning were active in Carthage in the seventh century and at the height of their activity ranged from Iceland to the Balkans. Great numbers of them invaded France in the ninth century, but Irish foundations had existed in France and Brittany since the seventh century. The forests of France, the valley of the Rhine, the ranges of the Appenines and even the region of the Alps furnish abundant vestiges to this day of monasteries and schools founded by Irish monks in the seventh and eighth centuries. In contrast to the breadth and diffusion of early Irish activity on the continent is the relative concentration of the early documents containing Irish Latin hymns, a circumstance significant only of the fate of libraries.

St Colum Cille's *Altus Prosator* appears in several sources other than Irish. Four of these sources are copies of works ascribed, in some instances erroneously, to Prosper of Aquitaine. Two copies are ninth-century manuscripts, another is of the tenth century, and the fourth is of the tenth or eleventh century. These Prosper manuscripts may be taken as witnessing to the knowledge of the *Altus Prosator* in the Gallican Church. A fifth non-Irish source is a poem by Hraban Maur, who plagiarized large portions of the *Altus* to round out the burden of his versified theology. The 'author' uses Colum Cille's system of rime throughout the composition, and thereby affords direct testimony that Hiberno-Latin rime of the sixth century was germinal to European rime in the ninth century.[23]

Two Germans who studied under Hraban Maur must be included among the foremost poets of ninth-century Germany. The work of one of these, Gottschalk of Fulda, reveals stanzas with patterned dissyllabic accentual rime:

> 1. ut quid iubes, pusiole,
>   quare mandas, filiole,
>   carmen dulce me cantare,
>   cum sim longe exsul valde
>   intra mare ?
>   o cur iubes canere ?

> 2. magis mihi,   miserule,
>   flere libet,   puerule,
>   plus plorare   quam cantare
>   carmen tale,   iubes quale,
>   amor care.
>   o cur iubes canere ?   RSLP, I,   p. 227

Though Gottschalk apparently lacked either the patience or the ability to sustain the rime scheme of his first two stanzas throughout all ten, and though he did not even secure dissyllabic accentual end-rimes in some of the lines of his last seven stanzas, he does succeed in ending every line of all ten stanzas with the letter *e*. Further, he seems to show some familarity with the Irish classification of consonants for riming purposes: the end-rime of the third, fourth and fifth lines in both stanzas quoted conforms with Irish practice. In succeeding stanzas, Gottschalk diverges, however, from this practice and to such an extent that he is revealed to have been concerned chiefly with assonantal echoes. This being the case, what is there to indicate that he had any conscious knowledge of Irish practice ?

He studied at Fulda, under Hraban Maur, who certainly knew the *Altus Prosator*. Perhaps better, he was at Reichenau before the end of 824 AD, and he was associated for some time at Fulda, from 827 AD, with Walafrid Strabo, a brilliant young poet who had spent most of his life at Reichenau, an Irish foundation that maintained its Irish contacts through the first half of the ninth century at least. Two of the finest specimens of Latin verse in the Irish style are included in a Reichenau manuscript of the ninth century, some portions of which date from the eighth century. These Irish poems are none other than St Cuchuimne's Hymn to the Virgin (p. 83) and St Colman Mac Murchon's Hymn in Praise of St Michael (p. 83). The coincidence of the appearance of these poems in an eighth- or ninth-century manuscript of an Irish foundation at which both poets had studied is striking, especially if the novelty of Gottschalk's rimes is as real as the extant poetry of his time and place makes it seem to be.

The Irish manner in Latin verse must have been known at the monastery of St Gall, which played a prominent part in the sustenance of mediaeval culture from the eighth century. St Gall manuscripts of the eighth century preserve poems in Old Irish, in the bardic measures. A St Gall manuscript of the ninth or tenth century preserves a hymn attributed to St Columbanus, the *De Vanitate et Miseria Vitae Mortalis*. This achieves a frequently accentual dissyllabic and sometimes trisyllabic end-rime between the second and fourth lines. Since the poem was (presumably) written during the early years of the seventh century, St Gall would have known it long before the date of the manuscript that preserves it. Considering the knowledge of accentual rime legitimately imputable to St Gall, or at least to some of its monks—many of whom, besides its founder, were Irish—the impulse which led the writers at St Gall to introduce assonance and rime, to an increasing degree, into their Sequences becomes less a matter of spontaneous creation than of conscious imitation.

The Irish and Welsh connections with Brittany and the Celtic race of the Bretons perhaps go far to explain the next coincidence to be advanced. The following stanzas are from a Sequence in honour of St Stephen by the twelfth-century Breton, Adam of St Victor:

> 11. pro corona non marcenti
> perfer brevis vim tormenti,
> te manet victoria :

12. tibi fiet mors natalis,
    tibi poena terminalis
    dat vitae primordia.

19. ne peccatum statuatur,
    his, a quibus lapidatur,
    genu ponit et precatur
    condolens insaniae;

20. in Christo sic obdormivit,
    qui Christo sic oboedivit
    et cum Christo semper vivit,
    martyrum primitiae. RCLP, p. 352

The following stanzas close Adam's Easter Sequence, *Zyma vetus expurgetur*:

19. Iesu victor, Iesu vita,
    Iesu vitae via trita,
    cuius morte mors sopita,
    ad paschalem nos invita
    mensem cum fiducia.

20. vive panis, vivax unda,
    vera vitis et fecunda,
    tu nos pasce, tu nos munda,
    ut a morte nos secunda
    tua salvet gratia. RCLP, p. 354

The structure of all the stanzas just quoted is essentially that structure of the sung dialogue verse from the *Táin*, quoted in p. 35. An irregularly rimed parallel to the last two of Adam's stanzas quoted appears in p. 10. Verse of this sort was studied by aspiring *filid*: analogous specimens appear in the Old Irish metrical tracts. Various forms of the three-line stanzas quoted from Victor appear in earlier Irish and Welsh poems.

Despite Victor's background, it is not insisted that he acquired either his predilection for accentual rime or his verse forms directly from Celtic sources; for all the elements of his technique had already been employed by earlier French poets. These earlier French poets had themselves been anticipated, however, by Celtic poets who had, centuries earlier, shaped the forms so seemingly novel to the continent even as late as the eleventh century, to judge from the laborious and uncertain handling these forms at first received.

Two devices of the sound-harmony of mediaeval Latin remain to be mentioned: continuous end-rime (monorime) within the verse-paragraph and patterned end-rime binding the first and third as well as the second and fourth lines of the quatrain. Both devices are richly illustrated in the *Antiphonary of Bangor* and in a number of other Hiberno-Latin poems that are preserved in continental and Anglo-Saxon manuscripts of the eighth to tenth centuries. Nowhere in Europe, save in Ireland, is there a decent approximation in Latin of the patterned accentual rime of the seventh-century *Versiculi Familiae Benchuir* until the twelfth and thirteenth centuries; and even then it would be difficult to find an extant item in which patterned end-rime on the accent joining the first and third and the second and fourth lines of the quatrain is sustained throughout the poem. As for monorime in Latin, it appears in works of other than Celtic authorship several centuries before the thirteenth, but not, in sustained verse, as early as the seventh.

On the whole, the highest achievements of continental sound-harmony in Latin are far short of the highest achievements of Irish sound-harmony in Latin. Of the Irish system, only the most obvious graces survived; and even these were very imperfectly comprehended. Thus, the sensitive and phonetically sound Irish rules for the rime of consonants seem to have been ignored in continental practice of the twelfth and thirteenth centuries. The interlinear links characteristically employed in the most ornate Irish Latin style were also either ignored as device or not even comprehended. The intralinear grace of internal rime was, however, familiar. On the other hand, alliteration was less frequent and purely sporadic. The end-rime—though very generally dissyllabic and often trisyllabic—was not, as a rule, consistently accentual; though, of course, dissyllabic and trisyllabic end-rime will usually involve accented syllables in Latin. The principle of regulating the syllabic length of verse-ends was not employed in the mediaeval Latin verse of the continent. In short, the continent and of course England had Hiberno-Latin models of sound-harmony to learn from but lacked a familiarity with the Irish system of sound-harmony.

The structural debt of continental poetry to Irish technique is indicated by the similarity of stanzaic forms common to the regular Sequences and Irish verse of earlier date. Though it is impossible to determine precisely how the contact between Irish song measures and the writers of Sequences was effected, the difficulty resides largely in the multiplicity of points of contact, direct and indirect.

The influence of Irish rhythm is significant, outside Ireland, only in the rhythm of the Anglo-Saxon Latin poetry inspired by Irish Latin verse. This influence faded as the accentuation of Latin became uno-accentual, in response to the triumph of the uno-accentual tendency in west European speech. On the continent, where accent had been modulated to Greek quantitative metres on principle, as in the verse of Ambrose, the Greek metres remained as a frame for accent even after quantity had been dropped as an essential concern for 'rhythmic' poetry. Consequently, and because of the underlying tendency of western speech during the eighth and ninth centuries to pass from bi-accentual to uno-accentual stress, the rhythm of Old Irish and of much early Hiberno-Latin poetry could hardly have impressed itself, save perhaps temporarily and sporadically, on the rhythm of continental poetry in Latin.

Celtic Affiliations with Provencal and Spanish

How far did the diffusion of Celtic versecraft extend? Are the Celtic parallels with Provencal and Spanish verse merely coincidence? Are they independent developments from an early Celtic source? Or are they late borrowings by Provence and Spain?

Spain was Celtiberian before the Roman conquest, and Provence was Celtic. The features of their verse that affiliate with Celtic versecraft could therefore derive from predocumentary verse, comparable to the apparent derivation of Old French traits from Gaulish or from a popular Gallo-Latin verse coloured by its Celtic domicile. On the other hand, characteristics of the Old French *chansons de geste* could have entered early Spanish verse. What, though, of the efflorescence of stanzaic forms in Provencal?

Provencal stanzaic verse is a relatively late mediaeval bloom. The mediaeval Latin lyric had already circulated extensively in both secular and religious forms. This lyric certainly incorporated various Celtic traits—notably accentual end-rime, transmitted through Hiberno-Latin hymns. But Provencal verse has traits of form and spirit not held in common with the mediaeval Latin lyric.

If Breton verse forms should have survived from the early mediaeval period, one could doubtless picture more precisely the background of Provencal verse. As it is, one observes that certain Breton and Welsh stanzaic forms are similar to certain Provencal forms. One also notes that Provencal verse is first documented not long after the vogue of the bilingual Breton storyteller had reached its height, with the circulation of the Arthurian legends throughout western Europe. William VII of Poitou (Aquitaine), a troubadour and one of the founders of Provencal literature, aided Arthurian vogue and its Breton narrators.[24]

Specific aspects of early Spanish versecraft affiliate with aspects of Celtic. In the *redondella*, the old ballad measure of Spain, end-assonance of classed vowels was admitted on weak stresses. As in Celtic practice, *e* and *i* made up one class; and *a*, *o*, *u*, another. (This distinction in vowel colour had been early reflected in the final array of the ogham alphabet.) On the other hand, Fiji verse displays a like regard for distinction of vowel colour. The early Spanish stanzaic forms termed *juglar* and *redondella* also employ mono-assonance for end-ornament, as in the Old French epic strophes. The fact that Fiji verse assonates in the same way does not discourage the supposition that a common Celtic background or a direct borrowing is involved. Though reserving an exploration for the future, we presume that the attested circulation of Breton and French minstrels in Provence and Spain dispenses with the need, that might otherwise exist, to postulate independent discoveries.

To sum up:

If the fruits of diffusion be tabulated, the Celtic contribution to the versecraft of western Europe will be acknowledged as substantial. Systematically accentual rime, both at line-end and internally, is the most obvious gift. In passing to England and the continent, Irish accentual rime was conveyed by Hiberno-Latin hymns. As their rime consisted chiefly in correspondence of identical syllables, its imitators ignored the possibilities of phonetic rime. Obviously, they were not taught its phonetic basis by the Celtic

churchmen whose hymns it graced, primarily because these churchmen were the users, not the composers, of the hymns.

The monorime strophes and quatrains of early Cambro-Latin
religious verse are a source of the monorime stanza in mediaeval
Latin. As Cambro-Latin monorime probably reflects a popular
usage of ultimately Gaulish and Brythonic antecedents with
Celtiberian affiliations, the continental appearance of Cambro-
Latin monorime would perhaps serve to confirm existing popular
practice more than to provide entirely new models. The use of
monorime stanzas in the Latin verse of wandering scholars possibly
represents a response to existing models of clerical Latin monorime
and to popular monorime as in Old Spanish and Old French lyric
and narrative.

Various stanzaic forms in mediaeval Latin derive from Celtic
verse. These forms include the accentually riming quatrains whose
end-rime patterns are a a b b, a b a b, and a a a b; the tercets
popular in Sequence verse, deriving from Wales and Brittany,
that rime a a b, c c b, etc.; the regular six- and eight-line strophes
of riming couplets, that derive from *Altus Prosator* (attributed
to Colum Cille); and certain less regular riming stanzas in short
line lengths and in combinations of line lengths. Mediaeval Latin
verse in turn served as model to verse in continental vernaculars.

The contributions of Celtic through the intermediaries of Hiberno-
and Cambro-Latin gave a decisive bent to European verse in a
direction that stimulated creativity for centuries. Ireland and
Wales must be conceded to be the fountainhead of European verse
in rhythmic stanzas that rime accentually.

Equally important, in terms of poetic value, is the Celtic contribution to European epic through the continuance and the diffusion
of Celtic versecraft. This contribution through craft survives
richly in the Old French epic, whose prosodic traits derive necessarily
from Gaulish when not from Welsh or Breton.

The Anglo-Saxon epic poems and fragments owe their redaction
and ultimate survival to the bent that Northumbrian culture
received from its Christianization in the Irish mode. Though
Northumbrian versecraft was retained with the language, *Beowulf*
is distinguished from continental Germanic epic largely by virtue
of the Irish elements that pervade its substance and its manner
of composition. (CSIH, chap. III)

Icelandic poetry blends Germanic and Celtic verse techniques. This blending began, and received its basic set, in the Norse-Irish kingdom of Dublin. The continuous participation of Irish and Norse-Irish poets in the development of Icelandic literature ensured the drift of its form and ornament towards a complexity and subtlety worthy of *filid*, involving the use of accentual end-rime and that panoply of device internal to the verse line whereby the interlacement, the knotting and the echoing harmony of consonantal sound create such webs of aural magic as appears in no other poetry save Celtic.

Generally, the relation of Celtic to other European poetry is like the relation of Celtic art of whatever form to other European art; to the extent that Celtic art was copied, it was a copying chiefly of the obvious and simple forms. The diffusion of Celtic versecraft throughout western Europe and its oceanic periphery endowed beneficiaries with rudiments and externals—accentual end-rime for Europe, but not Celtic phonetics; internal rime for the non-Celtic continent, but devices of consonance for Iceland only; simple verse forms for Church Latin and for its wayward scholars. Perhaps it was as well that the more subtle aspects of Celtic versecraft did not penetrate west European literatures for, without the discipline of the Celtic poet-schools, it is likely that a thorough application of Celtic practice to Latin and the non-Celtic vernaculars would have resulted in an almost complete constriction of what poetic voice the early Middle Ages could find. Irish and Welsh devices can bring the poetry of a language as near to a pure art of sound as may be achieved without sacrifice of meaning; but it is only a master that can move freely in the strict measures, and then only after years of dedication.

Part V : Conclusion

Celtic versecraft evolved from Indo-European archetypes, whose cadenced lines foreshadow the contours of archaic Irish epic-gnomic verse and of early Welsh epic-elegiac verse.

Indo-European verse accent was functional: it moved fluidly within the verse unit, for clarification of meaning and for emphasis. It could shift to match words with music or for other effects, as in Fiji verse. Such accentual shifts are attested in Vedic/Sanskrit (and in recent Esthonian verse).

With the advent of highly stressed speech in Germanic, Celtic and Italic, the archaic cadenced verse lines were pervaded by speech-stress rhythms which more rigidly defined the linear contours. The rhythms were first regulated in Celtic (and somewhat in Italic) by concepts relatively primitive—*word foot* and *word measure*—whose operation nonetheless ensured the emergence, within strophes, of verse lines uniform in syllabic count, in reflection of their rhythmic patterns.

Verse-line cadence, which had been established before speech stress had imposed its rhythms throughout the line, retained a central position in the Germanic-Celtic-Italic verse of paired stresses. The line of four strong stresses paired, with mid-point cadence, survived for many centuries in Germanic verse. In Celtic verse, this line appears more frequently in Irish than in Welsh; but early Welsh verse discloses frequently a line of three divisions (cola), rare in Old Irish, which echoes an Indo-European long line.

Germanic verse style, stereotyped at an early phase of stress rhythm, did not regard the rhythm of weak stresses. Celtic style encompassed the weak stresses by regulation—first *word foot* and *word measure*, then Celtic verse foot. Italic verse would perhaps have achieved comparable stress regulation, if Greek measures had not been adapted to Latin.

Celtic rhythm realized the potential of bi-accentual speech stress through the Celtic verse foot, whose rhythm involved an alternation of strong and weak stress complexes on a ternary rhythmic ground. This rhythm found expression equally in music and verse.

F

Celtic verse form attains a distinction comparable to that of Celtic rhythm, in a symbiosis of binary and ternary formal elements —incremental repetition and the refrain, triadic iteration within the quatrain, the exfoliation of triadic stanza from the Welsh epic-elegiac line, and the exfoliation of triadic quatrains from the Old Irish long couplet.

The heightening of formalization in Celtic cadence, stress rhythm and strophe impelled a corresponding formalization in the incidence of verse ornament. Initially, aural correspondences assisted in setting cadential boundaries. These correspondences (alliteration, suffixal chimes and repeated grammatical elements) first marked the beginning and end of sound complexes or sense units, and eventually pervaded the verse line in the wake of stress rhythm, engaging entire stressed syllables rather than initial or terminal sounds. With the emergence of analytic Celtic, the accented syllables tended to become also finals, through the loss of suffixal inflection; and intralinear verse ornament became, increasingly, accentual end-ornament.

The evidence of independent development in early Welsh and Irish verse includes differences in the cadential contours of typical verse lines; differences in the form of typical strophes and stanzas; differences in the kind, frequency, incidence and phonetics of verse ornament; differences in the frequency of identic as distinct from phonetic aural correspondence; and differences in the frequency and systematic incidence of ornament and accent. These differences —since they consistently relate early Welsh verse to ruder levels of rhythm, form and ornament—bespeak a conservative tendency and hence the probability that early Welsh verse retained an established Brythonic prosody. Otherwise, because of close cultural affiliations and its extensive Irish settlements, early Wales would likely have adopted Irish craft. That the hypothesized Brythonic prosody was comparable to Gaulish prosody is most strongly suggested by the remarkable parallels in technique between Old French and early Welsh verse—the parallels in Old French being attributable to Gaulish, when not derived from Welsh or Breton.

The end-ornament hypothesized for Brythonic and Gaulish, and actualized in Early Welsh, is non-accentual and, though phonetic, no advance over the simple phonetics common to Welsh, Irish and Germanic alliteration. Old Irish is, then, unique in the accentual incidence and the advanced phonetics of its rime, consonance and assonance. The advent of Old Irish rime and its variants can be dated to the centuries between the q-Celt invsaion of Ireland and the earliest documentation of Old Irish verse; that is, to a century between the first and sixth of our era—after the q-Celt invasion and before the adoption of Roman letters.

Special circumstances account for the unique aspects and the emergence of Old Irish rime and its variants: a strongly accented vernacular that has lost suffixal inflection in favour of initial, the cultivation of a passably scientific phonetics by learned poets to transmit orally an obsolete (sacred) language, the development of a popular riming poetry in the vernacular, the systematizing of the emergent accentual rime by learned poets, and their establishment of its phonetics. That rime and its variants were based in Old Irish on a unique phonetics rather than on simple aural identity leaves us in perpetual debt to antique learned poets for their attachment to Ogmios and to Vedas, long irretrievable (but perhaps comparable to those of India), which were once the sacred lore of proto-Goidelic.

Verification of the indigenous origin and development of early Celtic versecraft extends to poetry the concept of Celtic cultural continuity that has been well delineated recently in religion, law, social institutions and the arts of sculpture, metalwork, manuscript illumination and music.

The analyses of rhythm, form and ornament indispensable to our verification at the same time educe parallels and analogues in the style of craft among the Celtic arts of poetry, design and music. These parallels and analogues, noticed in passing, merit the most intensive scholarly treatment; for their correlation, and their relation to mathematics, may yet yield such knowledge as would enlarge the significance of antique suggestions regarding the role of *number* among the druids and the Pythagoreans.

The recondite *intensivity* of Celtic art denies its devotees the possibility of complete grasp. The subtle means completely engage the faculties; the secret remains secure. Françoise Henry senses the mystery, through close study of Old Irish design. The key to Celtic craft may be not only early number science but especially a philosophy that expresses a world view, a pantheism primitive and profound, that comprehends both Amorgen's Hymn and the far reaches of Johannes Scotus Eriugena.

What Mme Henry has written as to the early Irish design and ornament of sculptures, metalwork and manuscript illuminates also the essence of Celtic versecraft. Her words follow, in paraphrase:

In its early phase, Irish Christian art was a pagan decoration masquerading under the guise of an ecclesiastical art.   The ornaments used were the old La Tène spiral, Germanic animals, and half-disguised representations of Celtic gods.

Irish Christian art belongs to a very ancient past. The attitude of the artist toward an object, his use or arrangement of ornament, his sources of inspiration, and his reaction in the face of the world, all proceed from a long tradition, preserved and fortified during centuries of seclusion and independence.

There can be little doubt that spiral, interlacing, step-patterns, and stylized foliage are no mere 'ornament' in the modern sense. All of them, for centuries had been carefully spread over objects and on the surface of walls for the sake of their protective virtues and hidden symbols.   Ornament conceived in such a way is a sort of sacred riddle.   From a pagan cryptogram, it insensibly emerged into a Christian one.

The Celts organized ornament according to rules of their own whereby the love of intricacy, an inner regularity often hidden under a casual appearance, and the fear of too symmetrical compositions were essential motives.   Equality is generally replaced by equivalence.

One of the most fastidious and subtle systems of decoration ever seen is based on a definite unit of measurement.   The physical method, by an ultimate twist, is very often the result of an incredibly clever play of compasses or is based, as if on a scaffolding, on tiny grilles and regular networks of lines and circles—the use of geometrical instruments perversely turned to the construction of asymmetrical or irregular patterns.   It goes back very far.

In Ireland and in the Welsh-Cornish areas by the first century AD, deceptively similar curves are disposed inside identical frames. This tendency can be developed into a real method for cheating the eye. The circle interlacings with their suggestion of a discoid shape are the most elementary instance.   A circle and a three-fold pattern are combined in such a way that the fundamental discordance between the four sides of the square and the three-fold rhythm of the inner pattern is disguised in an appearance of perfect balance.

This finesse is of course strictly analogous to the development of triadic quatrains within the monorime *laisse* of *Y Gododdin*, and to the constant union of binary and ternary elements within the rhythmic pattern and formal structure of the Celtic stanza.

The magical conception of the world rests on a notion of man as not subject to scientific laws. Obedient to it, the Irish artist took refuge in a universe free of limitations. A vegetal pattern twined into a combination of curves is saved from becoming a stiff spiral by being transformed into a half-animal motif. These animals and plants are not only unheard-of species, they are also subjected to a strange transformism.

All the parts of this fantastic universe are interchangeable and can suddenly alter their form and merge into each other. Each being seems at once perfectly coherent, a finished individuality, and also able to partake of the nature of other beings and of inanimate shapes. This multiform and changing world where nothing is what it appears to be is but the plastic equivalent of that country of all wonders that haunts the mind of the Irish poets [the Celtic Elysium, the Island of Fand, *Moy Mell*—the happy plain]. With Christianity, God was substituted for the wizard of old times, but the notion of perpetual transmutations, of magical metamorphosis, remains unchanged.

The history of art has few nicer ironies than the Celtic ornamentation of scriptural manuscripts with design whose philosophic source is the pantheism of Amorgen's Hymn; or the Celtic panegyric of saints in verse whose web of sound derives ultimately from the inculcation of druidic Vedas.

When all is said of a culture, when its matter has ceased to be or to have meaning, what remains is its craft. Irrecoverable now is the capability of Colman's joy in the possession of a sword like Domnall's. Nor can the scriptures be discovered as if by revelation in books like those of Lindisfarne or Kells; nor can the harper be heard lulling the princess Gwennlian to slumber; nor can the magic be known of spells cast in jewelled strophes. But with study one can learn to stand in proper awe of Celtic craft.

The poetry, difficult to hear—like the illuminated manuscripts, difficult to see—can its art be useful still, even in English?

Our exemplar is also *envoi*—Douglas Hyde's rendering of O'Hussey's farewell, a use of verse to reveal the flesh made word:

> *Slowly* pass my Aching Eye
> Her *Holy* Hills of beauty
> Neath me TOSSING To and fro
> Hoarse CRies the CROSSING billow.

Notes

NOTES FOR PART I

1 Refer to EPP for generally reliable briefings on the verse of early China, Egypt, India, Sumer, Ethiopia, Japan, Polynesia, the Hebrews, the Esquimaux, etc. Useful larger studies include A. Erman, *The Literature of the Early Egyptians*, translated by A. M. Blackman (London, 1927); *Ancient Near Eastern Texts Relating to the Old Testament*, edited by J. B. Pritchard [second edition] (Princeton 1955); and QFC.

2 *The Battle of Maldon,* edited by E. V. Gordon (London, 1937).

3 Cato, *De Agri Cultura* [Loeb Classical Library] (Cambridge, Mass., 1934) chap. CXLI.

4 R. G. Tanner, 'The Arval Hymn and Early Latin Verse' *Classical Quarterly* (Oxford: The Clarendon Press, 1961).

5 The concepts of *word foot* and *word measure* are not discussed in the Irish metrical treatises. By the time of the treatises, the *word foot* and the *word measure* were long superseded as regulatory concepts. As such, they are of course not unique to early Irish verse; the *word foot* necessarily pervades early Chinese verse, partly because of the nature of the language itself; and early Hebraic verse (and also early Egyptian and Canaanitish), being based on symmetry of units, regularly discloses balanced statements, with equality in the number of words per line.

6 All MSS of the poem are defective. The portion of the poem quoted has not been edited.

7 I follow the edited version in SESS, pp. 31–32, in which Sigerson restored the Old Irish spelling and rounded out an occasional line, incomplete in single MSS but complete in a composite presentation of the MSS. An edited version with translation appeared as long ago as 1860—the work of Owen Connellan (*Ossianic Society Transactions* V, p. 232). Unrestored versions from three early Irish MSS were published in TMIV, pp. 35–36. In my quotation I have completed the third line from the end by adding *hir*, so that the line is now in harmony with all three sources quoted by Thurneysen; and I have altered the fourth line from the end also, for the sake of harmony with two of these sources and with the prosodic system of the poem.

8 Quoted in Thomas Fitzhugh, *The Indoeuropean Superstress and the Evolution of Verse* (Charlottesville, Va., 1917) p. 82.

9 The nature of early Germanic verse is discussed in HDV, which also introduces the previous literature on the subject. J. C. Pope, *The Rhythm of Beowulf* (1942), is highly useful on matters relevant to our study.

10 *e neges (ef)* is hypermetrical. See CA, pp. 105 and 108.

11 MMC presents decipherments of early harp music and a comparison of its rhythms and structure with those of early Celtic verse.

12 Thomas Fitzhugh, in a series of eighteen *Bulletins* published by the School of Latin, University of Virginia [Charlottesville], between 1908 and 1939, presented evidence and analysis of bi-accentual stress in early Italic and Celtic speech and verse. His studies appear to have been overlooked by the scholars most affected.

13   Nora K. Chadwick, *The Druids* (Cardiff, 1966).

14   John Cargill, *The Celtic Cross and Greek Proportion* (Chicago, 1930).

15   MMC discusses in detail the unique characteristics of early Celtic harp music, and indicates their impact on previous historical concepts.

16   The translation is from Kenneth Jackson, 'Incremental Repetition in the Early Welsh Englyn', *Speculum* (1941) pp. 307–308.

17   MEIM categorizes a number of Old Irish quatrains by their native names, rime scheme, syllabic structure, etc.   The data-base involved, however, is not comprehensive.

18   Wilhelm Meyer, 'Geschichte der alteste mittellateinische Rythmik', in *Nachrichten von der Königlichen Gesellschaft der Wissenschaften zu Göttingen, Philologisch-historische Klasse* (1913), p. 122.

NOTES FOR PART II

1   Though the linguistic relations of Celtic alliteration invite detailed discussion of sentence intonation, word boundaries, stress patterns, pitch, and quantity, we defer their discussion at this time as being not intrinsic to our case.   Further, we intend a coverage of these and related matters in a monograph tentatively titled 'A Linguistic Model of Predocumentary Celtic'. The evidence is sometimes uncertain and the field is controversial; but our approach will substantiate the antiquity of Celtic-Germanic alliteration, and its practice by pre-insular Celts (both p and q).   Indo-European analogues will be invoked to support a picture of linguistic states more complex than previous studies present; and the datings of archaeology on monuments will be taken as basic, thereby sacrificing the simplicity that marks some earlier literary approaches for the sake of a closer correspondence to fact.

2   Early Celtic ornament being based on correspondence between members of phonetic *genera*, the terms 'generic rime' and 'generic consonance' (first proposed by Professor C. W. Dunn of Harvard) can be most useful for identifying Irish and Welsh ornament as entities.

3   Consonant sequences, comparable to Welsh *cynghanedd*, are not compulsory in either early Irish or early Welsh practice.   Their statistical frequency and incidence indicate intent.   Consonance as an ornament is recognized in Irish metrical treatises of the eleventh century.

4   No exhaustive study of Celtic verse ornament has been published.   MEIM summarizes the rules of early Irish verse ornament, drawing primarily upon MPIM and Eleanor Knott's *Introduction to Irish Syllabic Poetry of the Period 1200–1600* (1928), and upon Bergin's valuable criticisms of MPIM in successive issues of *Eriu* (1916–1923).   MEIM should be read in the light of Brian Ó Cuív's review in *Éigse*, and of James Carney's comments in the Introduction to his *The Poems of Blathmac* (Dublin, 1964).   Following Thurneysen, MEIM rightly regards the ornament of Old Irish *alliterative accentual* verse as indigenous in origin, as against Wilhelm Meyer's assertion of its Latin derivation. Although unfortunately accepting Wilhelm Meyer's Latin derivation of the ornament of Old Irish *riming stanzaic* verse, MEIM refines this concept by stressing the role of Irish monastic experimenters in a supposed transformation of Latin ornament 'beyond recognition'.   It must be reiterated that the various assertions as to the supposed Latin derivation of Old Irish verse ornament in any of its aspects—whether made by Wilhelm Meyer, Kuno Meyer, Polheim, Zimmer, or Murphy—are in no case supported by exposition that even approaches the character of a demonstration.

5 See note 7, Part I, above.

6 See note 6, Part I, above.

7 *frigserat*, in line 6 of the poem and in the edited source, should be *frisgerat*. A Latin version of the prophecy supplies the beginning of a sentence missing from the Irish version: 'He will chant nonsense.' This would be inserted between the present fourth and fifth lines of the poem.

8 The satire on Bres has been edited brilliantly by Vernam Hull: see his 'Cairpre Mac Edaine's Satire on Bres mac Edain', *Zeitschrift für celtische Philologie* XVIII, pp. 63–69.

9 *Three Irish Glossaries*, edited by Whitley Stokes (London, 1862) p. 24. For another reading (*Yellow Book of Lecan*), see *Sanas Cormaic*, edited by Kuno Meyer, *Anecdota from Irish Manuscripts* IV (Halle and Dublin, 1912) p. 698.

10 Translation (partly guesswork) of a similar version by Eugene O'Curry, *On the Manners and Customs of the Ancient Irish*, vol. 2 (London, 1873) p. 218.

11 'Amra Senain', edited by Whitley Stokes, *Zeitschrift für celtische Philologie* III (1901) pp. 223–24.

12 The word *righthiar* is spelled *rigthier* in the source. The change of *e* to *a* is authorized by the other manuscripts, and by analogy with the other forms in *-ia*.

13 A brief summation on the date of composition appears in James Travis, 'Elegies Attributed to Dallan Forgaill', *Speculum* XIX, No. 1, (1944) p. 89.

14 The text of the poem in STP is restored, all MSS being somewhat corrupt.

15 For full discussion, see Alfred Anscombe, 'The Longobardic Origin of St. Sechnall', *Eriu* IV (1910) pp. 74–90.

16 For bibliography and comment, see James F. Kenney, *The Sources for the Early History of Ireland*, vol. 1 (New York, 1929; reprinted 1967 by Octagon Books, New York) pp. 258–60; and, for the poem's forgery, see CSIH, pp. 394–402.

17 End-rime, both stressed and unstressed, occurs frequently in a poem attributed to Columbanus as a work of his last years (d. 615). This poem does not employ the full system of Irish ornament. It was written at St Gall.

18 Robert Atkinson, *On Irish Metric* (Dublin, 1884).

19 For Celtic-Germanic prosodic affiliations, see James Travis, 'The Relations between Early Celtic and Early Germanic Alliteration', *The Germanic Review* XVII, no. 2 (New York, 1942), pp. 99–104; and also see TIRC.

20 HDV contains a good summary of early Germanic alliteration and an introduction to the literature of the subject.

21 TMIV, pp. 5–106, presents Irish prosodic tracts containing extensive indigenous terminology. Various terms from these tracts are concisely discussed in MEIM.

NOTES FOR PART III

1 Wilhelm Meyer, 'Die Verskunst der Iren in rythmischen lateinischen Gedichten', *Nachrichten von der Königlichen Gesellschaft der Wissenschaften zu Göttingen, Philologisch-historische Klasse* (1916), pp. 605–644.

2   Heinrich Zimmer, 'Über direkte Handelsverbindungen Westgalliens mit
Ireland', *Sitzungsberichte der Königlich Preussischen Akademie* (G. Reimer:
Berlin, 1910), pp. 1032–1044.

3   George Sigerson, *Bards of the Gael and Gall* [second edition] (London,
1907).

4   'Hilary's Hymn' appears in both LH and BACC.

5   Wilhelm Meyer, 'Drei arezzan.   Hymnen der Hilarius von Poitiers',
*Nachrichten von der Königlichen Gesellschaft der Wissenschaften zu Göttingen,
Philologisch-historische Klasse* (1909), pp. 373–433.

6   Thurneysen's usage of the terms *seadna mór* and *seadna* is observed,
since it is his theory which is under discussion.

7   The derivation of triadic quatrains from the epic-elegiac line of *Y Gododdin*
(CA, pp. 1–50) becomes apparent on inspection of excerpts quoted in Part I.

8   Wilhelm Meyer, *Gesammelte Abhandlungen zur mittellateinischen Rythmik*
(Berlin, 1905),

9   Rudolf Thurneysen, *Die irische Helden- und Konigsagen* (Halle, 1921)
p. 55.

10   The chief documents of Hisperic Latin were edited by F. J. H. Jenkinson
under the title *Hisperica Famina* (Cambridge, 1908).   The Hisperic technique
of distortion and obscuration is discussed in BACC, p. 151, and introduction.
MSLI discusses oghamic cyphers and the origins of Hisperic Latin and Hisperic.

11   More than forty of the names of persons that appear in Maro's parody
have a strong Celtic element, if they are not actually Irish. His illustrations,
parody verse marked by alliteration, patterned multi-syllabic rime, and
short verse units.

12   The sea routes between the British Church and Gaul were not closed by
the Anglo-Saxon invasions. See CEIS, p. 31.

13   Early Irish education is conveniently summarized in P. W. Joyce, *A
Social History of Ancient Ireland*, vol. 1 (London, 1903) chap. XII, and the
related references.

NOTES FOR PART IV

1   T. G. E. Powell, *The Celts* (New York, 1958) pp. 158–159.   Powell indicates
the potential fruitfulness of a comparative approach to Celtic prehistory,
utilizing the extensive detail of early Indian literary development.

2   Uno-accentual—that is, one strong stress in stressed words, as contrasted
with the earlier tendency towards the double stress.

3   Máire and Liam de Paor, *Early Christian Ireland* (New York, 1958).

4   Gradations are indicated in early law tracts and in the metrical tracts.
Consult *Crith Gablach*, edited by D. A. Binchy (Dublin, 1941); and also TMIV.

5   The *Laws of Howel Dda* (tenth century) specify Welsh legal distinctions
affecting poets.   A translation appears in *Myvyrian Archaiology of Wales*
(Denbigh, 1870), and elsewhere.

6   T. Gwynn Jones, 'Bardism and Romance', *Transactions of the Honourable
Society of Crymmodorion*, session 1913–14 (London, 1915).

7 Four of the six stanzas have eight lines of monorime. Various collects and antiphons in AB are in monorime stanzas of three, four and five lines. *Hymnus Sancti Comgilli* is in monorime stanzas of eight and ten lines each.

8 In early Welsh verse comparable to Irish *debide*, accentual rime is not compulsory. The rime of such Welsh verse is probably the ultimate source of the non-accentual rime in early Cambro- and Hiberno-Latin hymns.

9 The Latin mission to the Anglo-Saxons, despite Pope Gregory's initial adjurations, soon took a rigorous stand towards both paganism and the Celtic rite.

10 James Travis, 'Hiberno-Saxon Christianity and the Survival of *Beowulf*', *Lochlann* IV (Oslo, 1970) pp. 226–34, relates Irish Christianity to Northumbrian literature.

11 RSLP I, pp. 162, 167, 170–171; also MSLI. A strong case for the Irish origin of Hisperic is presented in Paul Grosjean, S. J., 'Quelques Remarques sur Virgile le Grammairien', in *Medieval Studies Presented to Aubrey Gwynn, S. J.*, edited by J. A. Watt, J. B. Morrall and F. X. Martin, O.S.A. (Dublin, 1961) pp. 393–408.

12 MMC establishes the Celtic provenance of the Reading Rota. James Travis, 'The Celtic Derivation of *Somer is icumen in*', *Lochlann* VI (Oslo, 1973), closely examines the lyric's Celtic traits.

13 *Layamon's Brut* (selections, edited by G. L. Brook: Oxford, 1963) pp. ix–xi. Layamon's use of rime need not have been inspired exclusively by Wace, and his use of alliteration with rime has abundant precedent in Celtic verse, as well as some precedent in Old English.

14 Whole poems attributed to Aneirin (*Gwrchan Adebon, Gwrchan Kynfelyn, Gwrchan Maeldderw*), as well as various *laisses* of *Y Gododdin*, are entirely in the form whose English variant occurs in Skelton and Shakespeare, and in West Country folk verse.

15 The stanza that concludes each alliterative strophe of *Sir Gawain and the Green Knight* has Celtic traits.

16 G. Turville-Petre, *Origins of Icelandic Literature* (Oxford, 1953) pp. 31–32.

17 Knut Gerset, *The History of Iceland* (New York, 1924) pp. 12–29. For some forthright, if general, views on the Irish influence and background, see Vilhjalmur Stefansson, *Iceland: The First American Republic* (New York, 1939), especially the introductory statement. The evidence of cultural interchange between Iceland and Ireland should be read against the background of Norse-Irish cultural interchange in Ireland itself. In this connection, see the studies by S. and A. Bugge (in Norwegian) on Irish influence and, for a general survey, A. Walsh, *Scandinavian Relations with Ireland during the Viking Period* (Dublin and London, 1922).

18 The parallels are documented by *laisse* and line in TPPD.

19 T. Atkinson Jenkins, *La Chanson de Roland* (New York, 1924) p. cxliv.

20 Sister Mary Hayde, 'Source of the Latin Trope' (unpublished Ph. D. dissertation: University of Illinois, Urbana, 1931).

21 *Analecta Hymnica Medii Aevi*, vol. LI, edited by Clemens Blume (Leipzig, 1908) p. 299.

22 Both poems are quoted in RSLP I, pp. 288–89.

23 For the authorship and sources of *Altus Prosator*, see LH II, pp. 142–46. For Hraban Maur's use of *Altus Prosator*, see Raby's works on Christian and secular Latin poetry (RCLP and RSLP).

24 Roger Sherman Loomis, *Arthurian Tradition and Chrétien de Troyes* (New York, 1949) pp. 18–19.

Index of Persons

Adam of St Victor 144, 145
Aethelwald (king) 140
Aethelwald (bishop) 141
Aldhelm 123, 139
Ambrose, Saint 70, 71, 72, 73, 84, 122
Aneirin, 120, 161
Atkinson, Robert 86, 159
Augustine, Saint 111, 121, 135, 136
Ausonius 121, 122

Bergin, Osborn J. 86, 158
Binchy, D. A. 160

Caesar, Julius 54, 111
Camelacus, Saint 73
Carney, James 158, 159
Colman mac Murchon, Saint 83, 84, 100, 144
Colmán mac Léníni, Saint 67, 155
Columbanus, Saint 141, 144, 159
Colum Cille, Saint 62, 74, 75, 106, 120, 123, 139, 142, 143
Commodian 121, 135, 136
Cuchuimne, Saint 82, 83, 84, 100, 144

Dallan Forgaill 58, 62, 117
Domnall 67, 155

Fitzhugh, Thomas 157

Gildas 138
Gottschalk of Fulda 143, 144
Grosjean, Paul 161
Gruffydd ap Cynan 119, 120

Heledd 117
Henry, Françoise 153, 154
Hilary of Poitiers, Saint 99, 100, 101
Hraban Maur 143
Hyde, Douglas 95, 97, 156

Knott, Eleanor 158

Llywarch Hen 117, 133
Lugair lanfili 24, 95

Maeldubh 139
Meyer, Kuno 2, 86, 95, 97, 103, 104, 111, 116
Meyer (aus Speyer), Wilhelm 2, 97, 100, 109, 110
Murphy, Gerard 39, 97, 105, 106, 108

Polheim, Karl 97
Pope, J. C. 157
Publius Virgilius Maro 109, 110, 139

Ó Cuív, Brian 158
O'Curry, Eugene 95
Oengus mac Tipraite, Saint 76, 84

Sanctan, Bishop 138
Sechnall, Saint 68, 69, 70, 71, 73, 99, 106, 159
Sedulius (5th cent.) 71, 84
Sigerson, George 97, 160
Snorri Sturluson 127

Taliesin 43
Thurneysen, Rudolf 2, 95, 97, 99, 100, 101, 102, 103, 104, 105, 108, 110, 157, 158, 159, 160
Travis, James 157, 158, 159, 161

Walafrid Strabo 144
Watkins, Calvert 13, 104, 108
William VII of Poitou 148
Wynfrith 140

Zeuss, J. K. 95, 97, 99
Zimmer, Heinrich 2, 97

Index of Verse

A solis ortus cardine (Sedulius) 72
Aliscans 133
Altus prosator vetustus 75, 106, 120, 142, 143, 149
Amra Choluimb Chille 58, 59–63, 94, 95
Amra Senain 58–59, 60, 62, 95
Amorgen's Hymn 5–6, 52, 153, 155
Amorgen's Incantation 6, 51–52, 102
Aucassin et Nicolette 133
Audite omnes amantes 69, 99

Battle of Maldon 2, 13
Beowulf 122, 123, 149

Canu Llywarch Hen 30
Carmen Arvale 8, 29
Chançun de Williame 133
Chanson de Roland, La 14, 132, 133
Charms (Latin) for foot pain 4; for sprain 4
Cētach conn na crīche-se 7
Christus in nostra insola 76
Coimdiu cāid cumachtach 10

De Vanitate et Miseria Vitae Mortalis 144
Deus creator omnium 70–71
Dialogue of the Despairing Man with his Soul (Egypt 2500 BC) 32
Doss dāile/dāl Temro 24–25
Druidic spells and satires 54–56

Elene 123
Ēnna Labraid/lūad cāich 4
Eo Rossa, roth ruirech 3

Finnsburg 123
Fo-chén Cét 11
Fo-chén Lábraid 11

Gawain and the Green Knight 124
Gilgamesh epic (old Babylonian version) 31, 32
Gododdin, Y 13, 14, 22–24, 33, 34, 36, 37, 50, 116, 122, 132, 135, 155

Heimskringla 127
Hilary's Hymn 99
Hymn to St Brigit 21, 64–67, 94
Hymn to St Martin 76, 77–79
Hymn to St Michael 83, 144
Hymn to the Virgin 83, 144
Hymnus Apostolorum 74
Hymnus Sancti Camelaci 73

Iascach múir 12

Labraid lūam na lergge 9
Layamon's Brut 124, 161

Māir drecain dā Ēnna 10
Māl adrūalaid īatha marb 9
Marwnad Cynddylan 36, 132, 133

Negro spirituals (See Spirituals, negro)
Nida dīr dermait 126

Ōr ōs grēin gelmair 9

Pangur Bán 37
Pearl 124
Praise Poem for a Sword 67
Prayer for Long Life 102
Prayer to Mars 2

Riming Poem, The 123

Sancte sator, suffragator 141
Sancti venite 69
Skeltonics 124; Shakespeare's use of 124
Somer is icumen in 124
Spirituals, negro 28, 29, 31

Táin Bó Cúalgne 6–7, 8, 35, 37, 50, 51, 53, 102, 139, 145

Versiculi Familiae Benchuir 21, 79–82, 146
Vie de Saint Leger 133
Voyage de Charlemagne 132, 133

Wanderer 123
Widsith 123

Index of Subjects and Terms

Accent. *See* Stress
Alliteration
  and *conachlonn* 6, 87
  binding (or link) 11, 50–51, 52, 53
  rules 45–46
  derivation 86–88
  Celtic-Germanic affinities 86–88
  (*See also* Rime and Consonance,
    Intralinear)
Alliterative accentual verse
  defined 3, 42
  exemplified 3–12
  its phonetics 43, 45
Ambrosian Verse
  characteristics 69–71
  Celtic emulation 71–74
  approaches to systematic orna-
    ment 71–74

Cambro-Latin Verse
  monorime 120, 149
  derivation from Welsh 98, 120
  influence on Hiberno-Latin 120,
    121
Caniad, caniad marwnad 16
Conachlonn 6, 51–52, 122
  and incremental repetition 6,
    50–51
  and alliteration 6, 87
  in Ausonius 122
Cynghanedd 38, 47, 48, 49, 125–32

Diffusion of Celtic Versecraft
  Irish-Welsh affiliations 120–22
  Anglo-Saxon derivations 122–24
  Norse-Icelandic derivations
    124–32
  Welsh-French affiliations 132–38
  Celto-Latin influences 138–47
  Provencal and Spanish deriva-
    tions 147–48

Entrance Rime
  defined 47
  exemplified 52, 55, 56–57, 59–60,
    61, 62–63

Genealogical Verse 26
  its combining of styles 63–64
Gosteg 16
Grammatical Parallelism
  and incidence of ornament 54–58

Hiberno-Latin Verse
  Ambrosian antecedents 70–71
  approaches to rime 71–74

Columban rime 74–76
  derivation from Cambro-Latin
    120–21
  Old Irish ornament in Latin
    76–85

Incidence of Celtic Ornament 50–67
  occurrence in earliest verse and
    styles 50
  conachlonn joined with incre-
    mental repetition 50–51
  binding alliteration replacing
    conachlonn 51–52
  rime, consonance, assonance re-
    placing *binding* alliteration 55–
    56
  parallelism of ornament and
    grammatical structure 54–58
  parallelistic ornament joined with
    binding alliteration 55–56
  ornament linking contiguous
    grammatical elements 59–63
  merging of styles in genealogical
    verse 63–64
  virtuosity in Old Irish ornament
    64–67
Incremental Repetition 22, 35
  and *conachlonn* 6, 50–51
  and *binding* alliteration 50–51
  in triads 29–30
  and refrains 30–32
Independent origins, manifest in
    verse of:
  Babylonia 31, 32, 115
  China 2, 18, 104
  Egypt 2, 32
  Ethiopia 2
  Fiji Islands, 2, 18, 24, 148, 151
  India (Prakrit) 18
  Israel 115
  Negro spirituals 28, 29, 31
Indo-European functional verse ac-
    cent 151
Indo-European long verse line
  survival in Welsh and Irish
    13–14, 35
  basis of triadic stanza 50
Inlaid (or heaped) rime
  defined 47
  exemplified 48, 56, 83
Interlaced rime
  defined 47
  exemplified 9, 57, 78
Internal rime
  defined 47
  exemplified 9, 33, 34, 77, 78

Intralinear rime and consonance
  sporadic occurrence in Celtic-
  Germanic *alliterative accentual*
  verse 89
  systematized in Celtic verse 90
  developed in Icelandic verse
    125–32
  (See also *cynghanedd*)

Juglar (Span.) 148

Laisse 116, 122, 132–38, 155
  (*See also* monorime and mono-
  assonance)

Monorime and mono-assonance, in:
  strophe 50
  hypothesized Gallo-Latin 136–37
  Cambro-Latin 120, 149
  Hiberno-Latin 120–21, 137
  Continental Latin 146
  Old Welsh 33–34, 36, 132–38
  Old French 132–38
  Old Spanish 148
Musical regulation 15–21
  and the *word foot* 17
  and the Celtic verse foot 18, 21

Ogham
  alphabet 113
  cypher for a finger language 113
  phonetic basis 113
  memorials 113, 114
  cyphers in *Book of Ballymote* 110
Old French epic
  verse line 14
  refrains 35
  incremental repetition 133
  laisse 132–38
Ornament in Early Celtic Verse
  styles and chronology 42–44
  (*See also* alliterative accentual,
    riming stanzaic, shamanistic
    verse)
  phonetic basis 43–44
  Irish-Welsh particularities 43–44
  rules: Old Irish 46–48
  rules: early Welsh 48–49
  incidence 50–67 (*See* separate
    entry)
  Hiberno-Latin ornament 68–85
  (*See also* Ambrosian, Cambro-
    Latin verse)
  derivation from structure:
    alliteration 86–88
    rime, consonance, assonance
      88–90
  development of Celtic phonetics
    90–94
  indigenous character of ornament
    94–96

Phonetics, Celtic:
  basis of verse ornament 43–44,
    90–94
  alliterative phonetics 45–46
  Celtic-Teutonic affiliations 2–3,
    86–88, 89–90
  riming phonetics 46–49
  Irish-Welsh differences 43–44,
    48–49
  relation to structure of ogham
    alphabet 113

Redondella (Span.) 148
Refrains 22, 27, 30–32, 35, 36–37
Rhythm in Early Celtic Verse:
  basis in stress or accent 2–3
  rhythmic regulation 2–14
  paired stresses 2–3
  word foot rhythm 3–7
  word measure rhythm 7–9
  rhythmic variation 9–10
  rhythmic determinants of syl-
    labic measures 10–12
  archetypal Celtic verse lines 12–14
  the Celtic verse foot 15–21
    occasioned by musical regul-
      ation 15–16
    musico-poetic analogues 16–18
  bi-accentual rhythm 19–20
  verse foot schema and scansion
    20–21
Riming stanzaic verse
  defined 42
  its 'new' phonetics 43, 46-47
  exemplified 35, 64-67

Saturnian metre 3
Sequence (French) 137, 142, 144–45,
  149
Shamanistic verse
  defined 42–43
  exemplified 52–58
Speech stress: bi-accentual, uno-
  accentual 117
Stanza types, Old Irish
  ochtfochlach 32–35, 104
  rannaigecht (incl. *rinnard*) 38,
    64–67, 104
  debide 37–38, 104–105
  (*See also* Structure in Early
    Celtic Verse)
Stress Rhythm, Regulation of 2–14
  (*See also* Indo-European verse-
    line cadence, speech stress,
    paired stresses, *word foot*, *word
    measure*, Celtic verse foot,
    musical regulation, syllable
    count)

Stresses, paired 2, 3, 4, 5, 6, 7, 13
    sequencing of 22–27
    and binary number series 26–27
Structure in Early Celtic Verse
    interplay of stress and gram-
        matical patterns 22
    emergence of stanza from paired
        stresses 22–26
    analogies between number series
        and verse form 26–27
    emergence of triadic stanza 27–32
        threefold iteration 27–30
        incremental repetition 29–30
        refrains 30–32
    emergence of stanza from para-
        graph 32–38
        triadic quatrain (*ochtfochlach*)
            32–35
        couplet (*debide, rinnard, ran-
            naigecht*) 35–37
    emergence of *amhrán* and *draig-
        nech* 38–40
    indigenous development of
        rhythm and structure 40–41

Syllable count and stress rhythm
    5, 6, 7, 8, 9, 10, 11, 12, 103,
    107–108

Verse ends
    regulated *word foot, word measure*
        10–12
    monosyllabic 7–8, 12
    dissyllabic 6–11
    trisyllabic 7, 10
Verse foot, Celtic 3, 15, 18–21

Word foot rhythm 3–7, 17, 18,
    104, 157
    word foot dimeter 4, 5
    regulated word foot 7, 8, 10, 11
    musical analogues 17, 18
    (*See also* Rhythm in Early Celtic
        Verse)
Word measure rhythm 3, 7, 8, 11,
    12, 157
    word measure dimeter 9
    regulated *word measure* 10
    (*See also* Rhythm in Early Celtic
        Verse)